Sales Unplugged

SALES
Unplugged

THE INVALUABLE "GO-TO GUIDE"
FOR BUSY B2B SALESPEOPLE

MICHAEL WALFORD-GRANT

NEW YORK

LONDON • NASHVILLE • MELBOURNE • VANCOUVER

SALES *Unplugged*

THE INVALUABLE "GO-TO GUIDE" FOR BUSY B2B SALESPEOPLE

Published in New York, New York, by Morgan James Publishing. Morgan James is a trademark of Morgan James, LLC. www.MorganJamesPublishing.com

Proudly distributed by Publishers Group West®

A **FREE** ebook edition is available for you
or a friend with the purchase of this print book.

CLEARLY SIGN YOUR NAME ABOVE

Instructions to claim your free ebook edition:
1. Visit MorganJamesBOGO.com
2. Sign your name CLEARLY in the space above
3. Complete the form and submit a photo
   of this entire page
4. You or your friend can download the ebook
   to your preferred device

ISBN 9781636981840 paperback
ISBN 9781636981857 ebook
Library of Congress Control Number:
2023935052

Cover and Interior Design by:
Chris Treccani
www.3dogcreative.net

Morgan James is a proud partner of Habitat for Humanity Peninsula and Greater Williamsburg. Partners in building since 2006.

Get involved today! Visit: www.morgan-james-publishing.com/giving-back

To Annie, and the memory
of our beloved son, William.

Contents

Acknowledgments

Thank you to Dave Swan my editor, and all the fantastic people at Morgan James Publishing, without whom this would not have been possible.

Preface

In February 2020, after more than thirty years working in sales for financial technology companies, I decided to start my own sales consultancy. I have always prided myself on my timing, but on this occasion, it escaped me. Within a month, we were all in lockdown here in the UK, and consumed by the Covid-19 pandemic.

However, tenacity and hard work have been the foundations of my long career, and I navigated my way through.

And now, here we are, in early 2023, living through an energy crisis, the Ukraine / Russia war one-year anniversary has just passed, there's a cost of living crisis, spiraling inflation, a Brexit hangover, a new king on the throne following the seventy-year reign of Queen Elizabeth II, and a replacement prime minister for one who only lasted forty-four days, and had followed the deposed and disgraced Boris Johnson.

As Mark Twain said: "Truth is stranger than fiction."

During some of my early assignments as a consultant, I produced "best practice guides" on a range of sales topics.

When putting them together, I worked through a dozen or more items I had collated over the years on the topic in question, and created a précis of what I considered were the "best practices."

As I was doing them, three things struck me:

- How much I do instinctively, without thinking.
- There were valuable skills and techniques I had completely forgotten, or had never come across.
- There are things I know, but don't always do.

If only I had a "dip in, dip out" guide, that I could refer to, to remind me of the best practices and tips on any particular topic. For example, a contract negotiation, or a morning of lead generation activities. It got me thinking…there is the potential for a book here.

A book that would be extremely useful for me, and hundreds of thousands of salespeople around the world, who are either:

- Overwhelmed with the sheer volume of information and materials available on any given topic,
- Feeling stale in what they do,
- Consumed by their role, and have failed to invest in themselves by keeping up to date with new research and new techniques, or
- Less experienced, and still learning their trade.

The thought of compiling a book didn't in any way faze me. During my 20s, when I was playing drums in rock bands, Boy George and Culture Club were shocking the public on *Top of the Pops,* and Margaret Thatcher was prime minister of England, I had compiled two books of specialist crosswords, both of which were published.

So the result of my endeavors is *Sales Unplugged.* Designed primarily for B2B salespeople, both experienced and those early in their careers, it is an easy to read, "dip in / dip out," aide memoire of sales best practices.

Why is it necessary, and what are its values?

The main reason is this. Research confirms overwhelmingly that the single most important factor influencing the outcome of a sales process is the salesperson. How they perform, day in day out, is therefore critical to their success.

Before I embarked on the book, I wanted to check that the size of potential market was big enough to make commercial sense. I had no idea what size I thought it would be, but I must admit I was blown away when I discovered there are an estimated two to three million B2B salespeople in the United States alone. I couldn't locate the global number.

So, drawn from a vast range of podcasts, webinars, books, blogs, and articles written by eminent experts, which I have consumed and saved over many years, the materials in the book are a stripped-down collection of curated best practices of what I consider are the necessary foundations and disciplines for consistent high performance.

To supplement these, in Part 2 of the book is *Stories From the Front Line.* This is a collection of stories, capturing a number of my experiences from the "front line," ranging from the dramatic, to the funny, to the deeply personal. It includes winning deals, losing deals, people conflicts, being sacked, ambulances, terrorist attacks, the day Lehman Brothers went bust, and enduring a formal performance improvement process. It takes place in cities such as New York, Philadelphia, Abu Dhabi, Vienna, Copenhagen, Dublin and of course my hometown, London.

And if there are a couple of conclusions I have been reminded of, both because of compiling the book and operating as a sales consultant, they are these:

- Keep everything you do as simple as possible, and
- Be proud of the sheer breadth of knowledge and skills you have acquired, to operate as a B2B salesperson.

Enjoy.

Sales Strategy & Planning

You have a new job or role. You have something to sell, maybe even a range of products and services. Your territory can potentially be segmented by type of company, which vertical industry they operate in, and whether they are large, medium, or small in size.

So which do you decide to prioritize and focus on, both in terms of the market segment and, if you have a choice, which product or service?

If the company has many existing clients and case studies, then analyze their characteristics, and draw out what, if any, constitutes **An Ideal Customer**; and then apply it to your role, and territory.

To further support this approach, below are the main types of considerations you will wish to consider, partly drawn from the best-selling author and speaker James Muir:

SEGMENT & PRODUCT/SERVICE COMBINED
- Market share
- Reference sites / proven examples
- Competitiveness

- Alignment with your sales targets, in terms of revenue, sales cycle, complexity of sale
- Depth and quality of internal support
- Alignment with your company's strategy (i.e., will you readily get support internally)

SEGMENT

- There is a compelling event that needs to be met, if so when / how soon
- There are strong industry drivers for change
- The segment does / does not have a culture of adopting the type of offering you have
- The ability and willingness of the segment to invest
- Size of the segment
- If there is an option of countries, then each will need individual assessment based on many criteria such as language, culture, travelling, competitiveness and more
- Is it a dynamic or static industry?

PRODUCT/SERVICE

- The pricing of the product/service, which size of firms can afford this, and what is the size of your sales target
- Does it effectively solve the customer's problems?
- Awards or endorsements from independent bodies

SUMMARY

The main ones to focus on:

- The size and immediacy of the problem you are solving (Problem).
- How proven your offering is in solving this problem (Leverage).
- Does this approach provide a realistic and best chance of hitting and exceeding sales target (Realism)?

Apply discipline, and do not waste time on prospects that do not match the "ideal customer" profile. Qualify them quickly or they will consume time and in all likelihood will fail to result in a positive outcome.

IDEAL CUSTOMER

Building on the above themes, in effect what you need to do is list your best customers, and then ask:

- What are their defining attributes?
- What are the common factors between them?

An Ideal Customer will therefore consider all of the above, in addition to aspects such as:

- Their reputation in the market / industry
- Who / whether they are influenced by, for example a research analyst, incumbent supplier, external consultant, or third party
- Attitude to risk
- How easy it will be to do business with them

Which Role Do You Target?

You have decided on the market segment and the product or service to underpin the sales strategy. Who will you target in the prospect company? What role, and what level of seniority? These will be your main considerations:

- Who are the decision-makers?
- Who are the budget-holders?
- Who are the likely influential people but with no decision-making roles?
- Do you approach IT, business, or operations?
- Who are the gatekeepers?
- Who will benefit most in the organization?
- Who is likely to be most receptive to your proposition?
- Do you have any existing contacts that will help you decide and guide you?
- What role and approach has worked effectively in similar organizations?
- Who will be defensive and protective of the status quo because it is a potential threat to them?

- Who will embrace the proposition, because it helps address a particular compelling event, business driver, or strategy?
- Is it an immediate issue or one lurking around the corner?
- Is your proposition leading-edge and pioneering or well-established in the market?
- Who will you appear most credible to?
- What level of seniority are you?

Do not assume that "going in at a senior level" and getting referred down is always the best approach. Sometimes it is, and sometimes it isn't.

That said, if you go in too low, then it can sometimes be difficult to get it raised at the appropriate level to count.

CONSIDERATIONS: THE DIFFERENT DEPARTMENTS

IT

If you have a solution that stands out because of its innovative technology, then IT groups may be a good target, but they rarely have a budget.

Sometimes they have enough influence to block initiatives or particular solutions, in favor of others. It depends on the particular culture of a firm and the strength of the individuals in senior positions.

If your solution is strong from a business point of view but has shortcomings in its technology, then you need to adopt a strategy that keeps IT out of the buying process for as long as possible, so a build-up of desire and momentum is created elsewhere in the organization.

STRATEGY

If, for example, you have researched the firm and you know there is a stated strategy to move in a particular direction and your product supports this need, then a strategy group or C level executive could be a good role to target.

Some strategy groups have a budget, some don't.

Strategy is typically set and driven by senior executives.

THE BUSINESS

They may have a set plan or strategy they are pursuing, and will often be the budget-holders.

Addressing their needs and demonstrating how your solution can help them compete against their rivals, enter new markets, or drive up revenues, should be well received.

They will typically be the most influential group in an organization in terms of what projects happen and which don't.

OPERATIONS

Typical areas of focus include cost of operation, process automation, and mitigating operational risk.

FINANCE

Anything that directly reduces costs, improves financial reporting and forecasting, and improves the balance sheet and the cost / income ratio of the company, will be of potential interest to this group.

SUMMARY

The main issues to focus on are:
- Who will benefit most in the organization?
- Who will be open to change?
- Who is likely to be influential enough to be able to progress the opportunity internally?
- For whom will it solve an immediate and compelling problem?
- What has and hasn't worked for your other clients?
- Who holds the budget, or has direct access to it?

Prospecting

This topic embraces many aspects: the approach, calling the prospect, when to prospect, leaving a voicemail, sending an email, approaching via LinkedIn, and so on. There is a wealth of information available on this most challenging and multi-faceted topic, including books, blogs, webinars, and research using neuroscience.

The theme underpinning all of them is:

Prospecting is the most challenging aspect of a salesperson's role.

There is no proven blueprint; there is no clear right and wrong way of doing things.

You will likely need to use a range of approaches (emails, LinkedIn messages, calls, eBooks, research, invites to events, news items of interest, etc), and a great many of them, before you either get to speak with your target or receive a reply.

People are "overwhelmed" with approaches, emails, and calls. That's why it is essential you grab their attention with a topic that "piques their interest." You need to trigger a response.

Tenacity and persistence are required, in large helpings. Why? Because:

Ninety percent of B2B meetings are set after six touches (according to a Harvard / MIT Study); most sales reps stop after two or three touches. The trend is also on an upward curve, and will increase from six.

The prospect needs to perceive you as credible, based on your various approaches.

Use "weasel words" when opening prospecting calls. Terms such as: "depending on," "might," "maybe," "perhaps," and "possibly." These are *non-threatening* words that hint you might have something of value for them, but you really need to ask questions first.

But before we embark on this journey, there is one topic that you must not forget.

The single most effective method of building your pipeline is with **Referrals.** The stats in terms of the engagement, conversion rate, and how much they invest, are off the scale more effective than any other form of lead generation. Especially "cold calling."

REFERRALS

- Use these as much as possible.
- Ideally, research the person on LinkedIn you wish to get to meet.
- If you have a mutual connection, then ask your connection to provide an "introduction," NOT a referral. There is a subtle but important difference. The latter implies they are endorsing your service.

- Only ever ask for one introduction, don't over-whelm them with more than this.
- Overcome your reluctance to actually ask for the introductions. Be confident, overcome your fear of rejection, but do ensure you have earned it before you ask.

MAKING THE CALL

Follow up emails and social media messages with a call.

Anticipate you may need to go through an assistant before speaking with a senior executive.

When they ask what you're referring to, make sure you have prepared what you are going to say; do not leave it to chance.

What you say to the assistant should be similar to the value proposition. We discuss value propositions in a later section; however, for the purposes of this section, a popular and effective approach includes:

- We help (the person you are calling), e.g., CEOs.
- Who are struggling with something (use emotional words).
- They may have tried something, and it didn't work.
- We may be able to assist, as we have helped similar organizations (their peers).
- I would like to explore this by taking a few minutes of his/ her time.

Rehearse what you are going to say on the call, especially if you decide to leave a voicemail message. See below.

If / when you get through:

- You need to pique their interest.
- The call is not for selling the offering; in most cases it should be for securing a meeting / follow up.

Do not ask if it is convenient; they have picked up the phone, so assume it is, even if they have interrupted a meeting they are in.

Anticipate objections to the proposition you have.

When objections come, such as, "we have no plans for this," or, "I am not interested," you need to keep them talking, and keep the conversation going.

You need to move them away from their reflex response, built up over time of being approached by salespeople.

For example:

Perhaps ask what would have to happen for the situation to change, or inquire whether they use a supplier service or one they have developed in-house.

If they are busy, and offer to call you back, resist and try and keep control and agree when you will call them back.

When trying to get through to someone, ring five to ten minutes before the hour and after the hour.

Research studies consistently suggest that Tuesdays are the most effective day for prospecting, followed by Fridays.

REMEMBER: You need a positive mindset; you have an offering that could potentially deliver improvements, you are not a pest. You are potentially providing a valuable service.

VOICEMAILS

Yes, you do leave them. Also:

- Pique their interest.
- Ideally align it with an email they can refer to and reply to.
- Rehearse what you are going to say; there is no room for ad hoc messages.
- Make it conversational.
- You are calling because you would like to "explore" whether you may be able to deliver similar benefits to others in the industry. Refer to "weasel words" above.
- Don't hide your number if you are going to leave a voicemail message. Be bold; you are not trying to hide anything. You may have something of value to them.
- Hide your number if you are not going to leave a voicemail, but be aware, some people will never pick up a "hidden / private number."
- Personalize the introduction if possible.
- Send a supporting email immediately after leaving a voicemail.

MESSAGING

A powerful, one-question formula that is popular and often effective is the question: "How would <something, something, something> help you to <reduce / increase> and in doing so <achieve a business outcome>?"

The above is in effect your Value Proposition. Its power is it helps the prospect visualize the business outcomes themselves.

It helps you make an impact, within the first 10-20 seconds. You need a "grabber."

That said, there is an art in ensuring it does not come over as contrived, and too slick.

Four things to focus on:

- Quantify the business impact (use % and ratio improvements).
- Use emotional, descriptive language (emotions trigger action, facts don't).
- Use contrast, current situation, and future outcome.
- Make prospects "think and feel."

GENERAL COMMENTS

After many unsuccessful approaches, be prepared to use the "Last Time" I will call option.**

Keep communication short and casual: "What's the best way to connect?" in an email, for example.

Using terms in communication that have been shown to work include: "Best in Class," "ROI," and, "We Work with Companies Like…"

If you do get a response, follow up as soon as possible.

If an incoming inquiry arrives, don't get overexcited; it still needs qualifying, and don't overwhelm them with too much material.

"**Last Time Call**:" Hi, I tried a number of times and I've not heard back. Either what we are offering is not a fit, it's a bad time, or you have other priorities. No problem. Won't approach again after this. If, however, you do want to explore the topic, then…**

KEEP CHALLENGING YOURSELF

How about those ten new companies you're trying to set up meetings with? You called them last week, then followed up with an email. So far you haven't received a response from anyone.

Mmm. That's interesting…

Perhaps a different message would be more effective. Could your subject line have caused them to not even bother opening it? Or could it be that you sounded like a product-pushing salesperson?

Review and change it if necessary, especially if the success rate is disappointing.

If you're struggling with negative self-talk, then:

- Write down a list of positive things about you and why people need what you offer.
- Then every time you have a negative thought, read at least three back to yourself.

The Prospecting Email

It is difficult to quantify the sheer volume of materials that have been produced, and continue to be produced, addressing this oh so important topic. Namely, the email you send to trigger interest, generate a positive response, and give you the opportunity to speak with a prospect.

I am not even going to quote the number of emails we salespeople send that are routed into Junk, ignored, or deleted.

However, if you follow these guidelines, you won't go far wrong. Furthermore, a great many of these best practices are backed up by extensive field research.

Never forget: Your email is one of a great many your prospects probably receive from suppliers, all trying to grab their attention. Plus they have a mountain of internal emails as part of their day-to-day job. So your message really must have an impact and make it as easy as possible for them to engage.

STRUCTURE OF THE EMAIL

Subject Line: It needs to be clear, describe the topic of the email, and get the recipient to open and read it.

Start with Hi or Hello.

Explain the purpose of the email.

Personalize it, relating to their industry (or an announcement by their company).

Trigger interest as soon as possible, with the promise of a prize if they read to the end. Demonstrate emotional intelligence and empathy: ***"...I will be brief and wanted to share something that I think will be valuable for you ... "***

Never use these most annoying phrases: "Not sure if you saw my last email...," and "Per my last email ... "

Also avoid terms such as: Please advise, Circling back, Friendly Reminder and Thanks in advance. Why?

Because: You don't want to guilt someone in a follow-up if they have not replied!!!!

Include a trigger event in the introduction if there is one. For example: We are running an event on a particular date coming up. You can also use a trigger event in the industry, like a regulation starting on a set date.

THE BODY OF THE EMAIL

Tell a story.

Make your prospect the hero if you can.

Use "you" not we; mixing you and I is fine.

Emotion drives action, so use emotive words that drive their desire to learn more. Use terms such as, "you may be feeling frustrated, worried, concerned, unsure," about something.

Show contrast between current and future, e.g. risk and resolution.

A popular structure is DIQ, Data Insight Question:

- State some facts backed by *Data.*
- Provide an *Insight.*
- Ask a *Question.*

The question is a bridge to the business benefits that could be realized.

Build in the need for urgency.

THE CLOSE

End with a call to action.

Sign off with: Thanks or Thank you (do not use Regards).

Include a PS with a question or a personalized observation (they are surprisingly effective in triggering a reply).

GENERAL PRINCIPLES

The email needs to be concise, clear and to the point. Use 100 words maximum.

Does it read easily on a smartphone?

Read it back yourself to be sure it is something you would read.

Mark Twain said it best: "I didn't have time to write a short letter, so I wrote a long one instead."

IF YOU GET A REPLY

If a prospect responds to the initial approach, such as, "Tell me more," or, "can you send me more information / your brochure."

What do you do?

Whatever you do, don't give them a brochure. Why not?

Consider following these guidelines instead:

1. Expand on the issue.
2. Share a case study.
3. Engage your prospect, perhaps with a recent blog or thought leadership piece.

Your objective is to secure a meeting or a chance to speak with the prospect, so you can establish their interest and judge whether or not this is a potential opportunity for you. The above is more effective than sending a brochure.

The Value Proposition

A value proposition is a clear statement of the tangible results a customer gets from using your products or services. It is outcome-focused and stresses the business value of your offering.

A simple model to follow, promoted by the best-selling author James Muir, amongst many others is:

Value Proposition refers to a Business Function = Direction + Metric + Magnitude.

Example: We help financial institutions improve customer retention by an average of 41%.

Prospective customers should be able to "visualize" exactly what value you could bring their organization.

Don't forget: Value Propositions may differ, dependent upon who you are targeting within an organization.

People are more sensitive and receptive to avoiding a loss than benefiting from a gain.

Once the Value Proposition is created, its subsets are Messaging, Your USP, Taglines and an Elevator Pitch.

MESSAGING / POSITIONING

Answering the questions below will summarize your proposition and messaging:

- Why Act?
- Why You?
- Why Invest?
- Why Now?

Avoid superlatives.

Statements made need to be defendable.

Focus on problems that trigger emotions, such as frustrations, worries, and bottlenecks.

YOUR USP: UNIQUE SELLING POINT

This should underpin whatever positioning you adopt.

THE THREE TESTS

- Unique to you (that your competition cannot do)
- Important to customer
- Defendable

ELEVATOR PITCH

Will be based on all of the above, presented in one or two sentences. Focus on business terms, solving problems, business outcomes and defendable statements.

If possible, your proposition is helping people and organizations rid themselves of a "headache."

Jill Konrath, an award-winning author, has published a great many articles on this topic.

Messaging

Your messaging needs to resonate throughout your engagement with the prospect and be a constant and consistent underlying theme. It will align with the positioning you have adopted for any given opportunity.

Messaging needs continual reinforcement for it to stick in the minds of the prospect, over what may be a long sales cycle.

It will incorporate elements of:

- Why Change?
- Why Now?
- Why You?

THE SIX ELEMENTS OF HIGH-IMPACT MESSAGING

There are many concepts around impact messaging. You won't go far wrong adopting these six elements from a James Muir article on high-impact messaging:

1. Driver / Trigger Event
2. Problem / Goal
3. Insight / Unconsidered Needs
4. Value Proposition / Outcome Statement

5. Feature / Mechanism of Action
6. Proof / Results

Driver/Trigger Event: External factor, causing the need to change. Difficult to control.

Problem/Goal: The priority / objective of the person/organization you are targeting.

Insight/Unconsidered Need: Something the prospect was unaware of (that you introduce), and recognizes the need to address it, and the added value your offering brings.

Value Proposition/Outcome Statement: The tangible results you produce/deliver.

Feature/Mechanism of Action: How you do it, your secret sauce.

Proof/Results: Evidence of past achievements.

SOME PRACTICAL TIPS FOR CREATING MESSAGING BASED ON THE ABOVE

Start with item 2, this will link to item 1, introduce item 3, then state the value proposition, with a statement of how you will do it, and what results the client should expect.

An alternative approach, which is just as effective:

Step 1. "My expertise is..."

Here is where you define your specialty.

Step 2. "I work with..."

This defines your target market.

Step 3. "...who want to..."

This is where you state the results you deliver.

Step 4. "For example..."

This further explains what you do.
Some examples:

My expertise is driving up sales revenues for technology suppliers in financial services. I typically work with FinTech early-stage and small companies that are looking to scale or enter a new market, and want to drive up sales and be more effective in their sales operation. For example, firms that have won some early deals, relying upon a Founder, CEO, or technology guru, that now need to implement sales best practices to be able to scale and replicate these successes.

"ABC Consulting is a market data consultancy, specializing in cost optimization. We work with financial institutions that want to reduce their cost of market data, and improve overall insight, governance, and control. Over the last five years, we have delivered average savings for our clients of 28%. Our premium service is underpinned by a "secret sauce," the blend of an advanced analytics engine combined with deep subject matter expertise."

If you are attempting to dislodge or replace an incumbent, then all your messaging and positioning needs to be focused on "reasons to change."

If your proposition is competing with the status quo of "do nothing," then the approach needs to focus on why "do nothing" is no longer an option.

The 1ˢᵗ Meeting

Since the Covid-19 pandemic and the impact this has had on in-person meetings, it's as likely your first meeting with a prospect will be over Zoom or Teams as it is to be in person.

That said, the core principles will still apply; you need to build **rapport**.

Breaking the ice: Be unpredictable. Resist breaking the ice by referring to their bookshelf or piece of art. Instead ask about something you researched. This shows you prepared for the meeting, and gives them an opportunity to talk about themselves, which everyone loves.

It is also a more natural bridge to a conversation about the business topic you are meeting about.

Preparation: Failing to plan is a plan to fail. It may seem obvious, but make sure you always do it, however experienced you are. And make sure it is thorough and considered.

The three questions that apply to first meetings and all sales encounters:

1. Why should this client see me?

2. What actions do I want the client to take?
3. How can I provide value at this meeting?

Researching the Client: Only by doing this will you be relevant to them at the meeting and focus on topics of value and interest to them.

Discovery: This is key for a range of reasons. It enables you to: qualify the opportunity; identify what value you could potentially bring, and draw out any "hot buttons."

There are a raft of techniques for Discovery, a popular one from some years ago being SPIN by Neil Rackham. For those not familiar with this: SPIN stands for **S**ituation, **P**roblem, **I**mplication, **N**eed.

Unconsidered Need: If you can draw out examples of unconsidered need, with an associated value, then you will set yourself apart from your competition.

CONNECTION, CURIOSITY, UNDERSTANDING, ENGAGEMENT

- Connection: rapport, trust etc (use small talk)
- Curiosity: what's most important to the buyer
- Understanding: the "implication" of the above
- Engagement: listen and help the client to achieve their desired outcomes, both personal and business

See Meetings: stressing the importance of advancing a sale.

Handle the question: "**How much does it cost**?" very carefully if you have not yet established the value of the offering.

That said, the sooner you establish whether or not their expectation of budgets is in the correct ballpark for what your service typically costs, the better; this avoids pursuing lost causes.

Don't be fixated by the statement: "We only have this budget available." If you can demonstrate value, and there is desire from the buyer, then if a higher budget is required, there are many ways to overcome their statement.

Establishing your credentials: For you to realistically advance the opportunity, you need to establish trust and demonstrate knowledge. You need to be credible. You need to begin to build a relationship.

Where are they on the **Buying Cycle**? Establishing this will assist you in the positioning and messaging you use, and in qualifying the opportunity.

Are **external consultants** involved?

How do **decisions** get made and where does this person sit within the **organization**? Who is **sponsoring** the opportunity? Is it part of a strategic program?

Meeting Management & Advancing the Sale

Meetings come in all shapes and sizes. Some include a presentation and maybe a demonstration of your offering, while others may be walking through a commercial proposal, for example. Some may be a scheduled call or online meeting.

There are some best practices that apply to them all.

PREPARATION

Set an agenda, or list of topics for the meeting. It provides structure, discipline and focus for all who are attending, which will improve the likelihood of positive outcomes.

Define a meeting objective with a focus on outcomes that the prospect wants to achieve from it.

Make the agenda and topics as compelling as possible to attract maximum attendance, so the right people attend and enable the sale to advance.

Always allow sufficient time at the end for actions and next steps, so the opportunity can be advanced.

Always summarize the meeting with actions, next steps, timescales AND take the opportunity to schedule the next meeting while you have everyone's attention.

As with all sales encounters, ensure the attendees leave feeling they have learned things and you have added value.

You will have objectives for the meeting. So prepare the right questions to ask.

When selling an idea, if your questions lead the attendees to suggest the idea themselves, then all the better.

Your objective is to progress the sale, which will move the opportunity forward.

The acid test of progression is whether there is an agreed action from the prospect that requires some effort to complete.

Plan your ideal outcome, and fallback ones.

Building and maintaining momentum, needs to be an on-going focus.

The concept of progressing an opportunity applies to all sales encounters, not just a meeting or call.

Prior to a meeting, ask yourself these four questions:

1. What do I need to *find out* to improve my chances of winning the deal, or further qualifying the opportunity?
2. What do I want them to *know?*
3. What do I want them to *do?*
4. How do I want them to *feel?*

CLOSING A MEETING

Always take control of the next step. Never ask them "How do we proceed from here?" Take control. These "Closing" questions will help progress the opportunity:

"Does it make sense to…?" tests how ready they are, and where the prospect is on the buying process.

"Clients typically do xxx at this stage, does it make sense for us / you to do the same?" A "No" does not shut the door on the opportunity.

"What is a good next step then?" The answer will be valuable insight into where they are on the Buyer Cycle.

As above, have fallback questions and outcomes in mind, so momentum is maintained.

A Continuation is a commitment to keep engaged but with no specific actions that will continue to move the opportunity forward with momentum or target timescales.

Creating trust accelerates sales. Attempting to close or advance opportunities faster than clients are ready for erodes trust. Closing gambits also erode trust.

The well-respected author Neil Rackham defined the terms referred to in this section in the following way:

Close—a firm commitment to buy. The signed order marks the transition from evaluation to actual ownership.

Advance—a significant action that requires energy by the client (either in the call or right after it) that moves the sale toward a decision.

Continuation—a situation where the sale will continue yet no specific action has been agreed upon by the customer to move forward.

Closing is easier when you achieve consistent Advances after every encounter.

Qualifying an Opportunity & the Probability of Success

For the opportunities in your pipeline, there will be a great many factors that will affect the qualification and probability of success.

The probability of success will evolve over time as the buying process develops.

Qualification needs to be an ongoing activity.

The factors below refer to an opportunity in the pipeline.

Before speaking about items in the pipeline, let's make sure we are all clear what the difference is between items in the funnel and in the pipeline. Items typically move from funnel to pipeline once Awareness, Interest, Desire, and Action have been demonstrated by the customer (AIDA).

These questions might be relevant at the outset, or on an ongoing basis during the sales process:

- Is it always you doing the running?
- Do they deliver on their actions?
- Is there an incumbent that needs to be dislodged?

- Have they considered change before and decided not to act?
- How disruptive will the change be?
- How strong is the ROI?
- Is it strategically important?
- How engaged are the business sponsors / budget holder?
- What is the prospect's perception of the risk of your offering?
- Do you have an internal coach, or champion, and what influence internally do they have?
- How does your offering match the culture of the company in terms of: early adopter, fast follower, laggard?
- How strong is the personal motivation of the key stakeholders?
- Will the solution negatively impact anyone, and if so what power / influence do they have?
- Is there a compelling event, and how strong are the business drivers?
- What is the strength of the competition?
- Do you have a USP, and if so, what is its relative strength (through the eyes of the prospect)?
- What are the consequences of "doing nothing or applying a short-term workaround?"
- Have you met all the key players; are you being denied access?
- Was the opportunity triggered by a cold approach from you or did the firm approach you?

- If the engagement is a formal process including an RFI or RFP, did you influence the scope and selection criteria? If you didn't, did your competition?
- Is there a third party involved, in full view or behind the scenes, and if so, what preferences do they have?
- Do you have proven cases to match what is being proposed?
- Has a colleague reviewed the opportunity and offered a view?
- How close to your "ideal customer" is the prospect?
- Are they willing to invest in a Proof of Concept?

WHAT THE PROSPECT / CUSTOMER WILL BE THINKING EVERY TIME THEY INTERACT WITH YOU

- How simple is your proposal to implement? Will it take lots of time and effort, and be disruptive internally?
- Does this person / company provide value?
- Is this aligned with what we are trying to achieve strategically?
- How urgent is it? How important is it to us?
- What value could this supplier provide in the future, or should this be viewed as a one-off transaction?

Presentations

This Section needs to be read in conjunction with the best practices of managing a meeting. Avoid "Death by PowerPoint." Consider the **10-20-30 rule**:

- 10 slides maximum
- 20 minutes presentation time (even if the meeting is one hour)
- 30 is the font size so words are kept to a minimum and the meeting is conversational

Adopt the following key principles:

- Have a recurring theme that runs throughout the materials. This will be based on the positioning of the offering, the value proposition, and the messaging.
- A picture paints a thousand words, so use graphics and pictures as much as possible.
- Do not overload slides with too many words. Use bullet points (maximum of four).
- Limit the scope of what you cover. Do not necessarily cover every nuance of the offering. Limit it

to the areas that will make a difference and achieve the objective of the materials: namely, to convince the prospect to continue to engage with you and move to the next stage of the buying process.

Why do you need an underlying theme, and core messages recurring throughout the presentation materials? Because people forget up to 90% of what you tell them within two days. You need to influence the 10% they remember. This method will help.

Never start a presentation talking about your company.

Begin dramatically, tell a good story, make a point, and deliver a benefit. This is "the attention grabber."

Know your audience, their role, and responsibilities, so you know what materials to include, the topics to cover, and the outcomes you want to achieve.

Establish your credentials by providing your insight into the business challenges and drivers in the target market.

Tell stories to make a point.

Use case studies as much as possible.

Structure the materials to encourage questions, debate, and interaction. If you can ask questions that get the audience to ponder and reply with, "that's a good question," then this is a big plus. It probably means you have unearthed an "unconsidered need."

Use consistent graphics and do not mix up photos, cartoons, images etc.

Use positive images and graphics because they prime positive emotions and feelings.

The presentation structure is designed to get the audience to arrive at the conclusion you want, whether that's a decision or a desire.

A "formal meeting" presentation structure that can work, depending upon your proposition, is as follows:

- Introduction
- Business Drivers, Insights, & Market Trends
- Overview of the Offering
- Case Studies
- Business Case for Change
- Summary / Close

End the presentation by addressing the following four questions:

- Why Act?
- Why Invest?
- Why With You?
- Why Now?

The time you spend on each topic will depend on where the prospect is in their buying process. If they need convincing to consider the concept at all, you will need to focus on Business Drivers, Insights & Market Trends, whereas if they are already convinced they need to do something, then a focus on "Why You," will be appropriate.

Leave enough time to have a wrap up with a summary and an agreement of next steps. Stress this if a colleague is covering some of the meeting with you, so they do not overrun.

Preparation time: If you know your subject, then you will be surprised how little time you need for rehearsing the content. Focus more on delivery, timing, and structure.

Commercial Proposals

Most commercial proposals are submitted as part of the buying process, at the stage by which you have:

- Engaged
- Created interest
- The client has acknowledged a need and interest, and
- Has requested a commercial proposal

Don't forget when submitting a proposal, that, "Pricing stands for 30 or 60 days, after which you reserve the right to modify it."

If possible, offer three choices, and lead the buyer to the one you want them to select; it makes them feel they made the choice.

When "leading" a client to a particular option, you can use wording such as: "most of our clients select this one," or, "clients with a similar profile to you."

KISS: keep it simple, stupid. Avoid complexity in the pricing model if possible.

Configure packages of modules or products that align with how they run their business. Apply business names to the packages.

Bundled packages can work well. Provide breakdowns of the items in the package, to demonstrate how much value you are providing. However, do not list the individual item pricing; the price is a "bundled packaged" price. This helps you to protect and defend the price.

Including optional modules and services can be effective. This approach can avoid "sticker shock" if your products / service / packages carry a premium price.

Ensure there is a buffer for negotiations. Deliberately build one in. For example, apply limits to certain items like the number of users, volumes, transactions, or hours of support.

Offering discounts / concessions tied to a "if we sign by the end of the month / quarter" rarely work. Don't do them, or be very wary of them.**

Consider how the organization can budget for CapEx and OpEx; one-off fees and ongoing. Do you know which "pot" your project will be drawn from?

If possible, don't just send the Proposal, always arrange a meeting to go through it. This helps avoid misunderstandings, plus you can gauge a reaction and provide an opportunity to Advance the sale. (This may not be possible during a formal RFP process.)

Don't offer a commercial proposal; wait for the prospect to request one. Why? It is a further test / qualification technique of whether the prospect is serious.

If possible, include a model and examples of a typical business case for investment for ROI purposes. Better still, apply it to the prospect's specific circumstances.

Price is important but rarely the primary selection criteria. This applies both in business and our personal lives.

That said, you should do all you can to avoid "sticker shock."

What you are selling is hopefully value-based pricing.

Detail in your commercial proposal the value it delivers to the customer, not just the cost of providing the service or solution.

Where possible, calculate the cost of their pain, show how you can remove it, then sell your product at a price lower than that cost.

If there are trigger amounts that require higher levels of approval within both your organization and the client organization, then bear this in mind and price accordingly.

Never use the term "List Price." It invites the buyer to negotiate a discount.

The "assessment of risk:" This is the client's perceived risk of selecting your proposal. Risks include the likelihood of hitting a return on investment, you the supplier, the product / service / technology, the project. Do not shy away from the topic. Address it head on.

Once you have finalized the commercial proposal, sit back and apply the **sniffer test**:

- Does it smell right?
- Is it too high, too low?
- Does the solution offer good value?

- Can the prospect build a coherent and realistic business case?
- Can you defend the price?

When writing the Proposal, always assume it will be distributed internally within the prospect's organization, and will be read by people that have little or no background or context.

A Proposal document structure, if you are not following a set template provided by the prospect, should include all of the following:

- Executive Summary
- Statement of the Requirements
- The Solution: How your offering meets the requirements
- Investment Section, including outline implementation timetable
- Building a Business Case for Change / Investment
- Summary / Next Steps (which should include a future vision)
- Appendix, including:
  - » Product / Service Overview
  - » Case Studies
  - » Company Profile
  - » Articles / Press Releases

OVERRIDING PRINCIPLE

- Keep the size and length of the main Proposal down (use the Appendix for supporting information so the core Proposal is not unnecessarily long).
- Keep the language simple.
- Use the Appendix for supporting information and generic text.

THE PROPOSAL FROM THE PROSPECT'S POINT OF VIEW

The reader will be reading and evaluating a Proposal with the following in mind:

- Does it meet our needs?
- Do these people understand my business?
- What is the project risk?
- How will the organization benefit, and what is a plausible return on investment?
- Does this initiative align with other company programs?
- What will it cost, both initially and on-going?
- Will this company be in business in a few years' time to support me, and if not, what are the consequences?
- Is there the potential for a long-term partnership with this supplier?
- How do I personally benefit if the project goes ahead with this supplier?

** One way of exploring the feasibility of this topic without exposing yourself to a discount is the question:

"Hey, this is just an idea because I have seen it happen occasionally with other deals. There may be some concessions available if you were to sign by 'the end of the month / end of the quarter.' Might this work from your end in terms of the decision-making process? If so, I can check things out with my management."

The Sales & Buying Process

THE BUYER'S JOURNEY

Depending on your age and experience and what you sell, the purchasing of products and services has undergone a revolution over recent years. In particular, technology-based offerings.

Increasingly it is being referred to as a Buyer's Process and not a Sales Cycle.

There are a great many reasons for this, all of which have led to the situation whereby buyers are dictating the engagement process substantially more than they ever have done in the past.

And this will continue for the foreseeable future.

However, there are many best practices a salesperson needs to adopt and keep in mind, to ensure they align themselves accordingly.

SALES CYCLE REVOLUTION: SUMMARY

The fundamental change is your role as a salesperson is not to sell, but to help the buyer to buy.

You will be focusing on the business drivers, solutions, and outcomes, and less on the specifics of the system.

It is likely to be a medium-to-long sales cycle, and you acknowledge the importance of seeing the big picture, focusing on needs at all times, and earning the right to access.

You need to be a trusted advisor who provides valuable insight.

You need to assist the prospect to build a compelling business case for change.

All buying decisions will be business decisions.

Keep reminding yourself of these four things (extracted from the widely read book *SNAP*, by Jill Konrath):

- Keep it **S**imple
- Be i**N**valuable
- Always **A**lign
- Raise **P**riorities

The Buying Process splits into three broad areas: ***Awareness, Evaluation and Decision***.

Messaging and positioning during each stage need to be different.

A failure to match stage and messaging will undermine your impact.

For example, during the Awareness phase your role is to educate, provide insight into what peers are doing, and help them to establish whether they have a problem, and if so, how big it is.

During the Evaluation phase you need to sell them on how you can help them solve their problem, and why you are the best choice.

The Decision stage is when you help them build a business case and calculate the ROI.

The pace of the sale is important; it needs to be at the speed the organization operates at. If you try and go too fast, you will slow it down instead.

Regulate the amount of information you share, so it is not too much to digest, and overwhelming.

It is also valuable to hold items back so if there is a lull in the process, you have something of interest and value to share as a meaningful means of "keeping in touch," and avoiding the salesperson's anxiety of "it's all gone silent."

By building a reputation for consistently "adding value," the prospect will "want to" remain engaged with you during their internal-facing periods.

Advancing the sale and closing is not what the salesperson does to the client, it is a joint activity.

Research shows that the salesperson, their experience, and how they conduct themselves through the sales and buying process is more influential on the sales outcome than any other factor, and by quite a margin!!!!!!

Confidence, Competence and Content are all critical for sales effectiveness!!!!

If you are attempting to dislodge or replace an incumbent, then all your messaging and positioning need to focus on "reasons to change."

If your proposition is competing with the status quo of "do nothing," the approach needs to focus on why, "do nothing is no longer an option." **

When you increase the complexity of the decision, you decrease the likelihood of closing the sale. To help your prospects move forward, give them less to choose from. Keep it as simple as possible.

Sometimes your internal sponsor won't be familiar with their internal decision-making process and the techniques required to move proposals through their organization. Take the lead and coach them through it, providing materials and knowledge.

Identify and secure a coach if at all possible.

Your prospect is probably overworked, short of time, and frazzled.

Complexity grinds them to a screeching halt.

When they sense that the effort required will make their lives more complicated, they call it quits—even if the change would have been good for them.

Once again, referring to the aforementioned Jill Konrath book, **the opportunity will descend into the D Zone**.

When you are in the D Zone, your sales are **Delayed** temporarily or **Derailed** permanently, as customers **Default** to the status quo.

That's why pacing the sale and keeping it as simple for them as possible is so important.

POWER AND THE ORGANIZATION YOU ARE TARGETING

There are six types of power that exist in an organization:

- Hierarchy [formal]
- Influence [informal]
- Control of internal resources
- Owners of knowledge & skills
- Control of the operating environment
- Involvement in strategy

Try to match the various stakeholders involved in the buying process to one of the six, or in some cases more than one.

Identify decision makers, budget holders, and the decision-making process as soon as possible.

Why do people buy? Meeting their business needs is of course key, but it is typically not enough. You need to serve their individual needs too.

It's a personal gain that satisfies an individual buyer's perceived self-interest.

Create and maintain a sales or deal plan once an opportunity is qualified and of sufficient value to justify it.

Momentum is key for a range of reasons. The main one is because change is constant. Every day the opportunity does not progress increases the risk that it never will.

Frustrated that the prospect is not moving at the pace you would like? One way to get a shared vision is through visualization. Ask the customer when they envisage the project will go ahead. Their answer will make it more real and visible for them and increase the likelihood of them taking actions aligned with their aspirations.

Keep challenging yourself and the situation you believe to be in; avoid "happy ears."

Look out for individuals referred to as "empty suits" in the prospect's organization, and indeed your own. These are people that attend meetings and calls, commit to do something, and then don't. They also have little or no internal influence. Find ways to bypass them.

Studies show comprehensively that success in selling is directly linked to the number of questions asked during the process and meetings. Keep asking questions, especially those that uncover need, and attitudes.

The profile of successful salespeople:

- They analyze their own methodology.
- They are constantly reassessing sales strategy and tactics, and which ones improve competitive edge.

The Buyer is constantly evaluating supplier propositions in the following terms:

1. Commercial
2. Strategy
3. Politics
4. Risk
5. Compliance

The "Buyer" is a team of people adopting ***consensus decision*** making, so all interested parties and stakeholders need as many of their needs addressed as possible.

You as the salesperson will often not be aware of the alternatives available to the buyer, especially internal work-arounds. In other words tactical solutions to get the prospect through whatever situation they are trying to resolve. Keep a lookout for them.

Assume your contact will leave the company, get downsized, or go on unexpected medical leave; so develop contacts and relationships as widely as possible.

Make it as easy as possible for the prospect to deal with you.

If you are sending a document that you want the client to read, then tell them what you are sending, the context, and on which page to find the section they will be particularly interested in. Don't be lazy and just send the document without promoting its values to advance the sale.

** Repeated in Messaging.

The Business Case for Change / Investment

The terms "change" and "investment" are interchange-able depending upon the circumstances and context of what is being proposed.

It is your responsibility to help your prospect buy. A core part of this is assisting them with building a business case and return on investment. Act as their "trusted advi-sor."

Remember, your proposal is not necessarily in compe-tition with another supplier, but with other projects being proposed from other departments. You need to arm your sponsor with the most compelling case possible.

The main elements of the business case must address both quantifiable and non-quantifiable factors. The main ones are likely to be drawn from the following:

- Reducing costs: both one-off and on-going total cost of ownership.
- Increasing revenue.
- Gaining market share.
- Improving profitability.

- Reducing operational risk.
- Improving:
  - » Productivity
  - » Time to market (of new services)
  - » Business agility
  - » Customer service
  - » Customer loyalty
  - » Staff retention
  - » Governance and control
  - » Consistency of service

- Lower training costs.
- Quicker value to market.
- Impact of change on internal operations and systems.

All the above will be underpinned by the USP and Value Proposition.

In effect, if the prospect "does nothing," then the consequence will be they are less likely to reduce operational risk, gain market share, improve profitability, and so on.

Apply real numbers and projections where they are available.

Customers require a faster return on investment than ever before, so focus on this. Even if a prospect acknowledges long-term, strategic value, look for quick wins, with a short return on investment.

This can build confidence among the stakeholders to continue with the program.

Buyers are increasingly knowledgeable on what constitutes a realistic business case, so ensure your projections are credible, not wishful thinking.

Complementary to the above are the Business Outcomes of implementing your solution, which are often targeted to Operations Management and Senior Executives. These factors include:

- Improved business agility
- Lower cost of ownership
- Lower operational risk
- Improved operational control and visibility
- The foundations for growth and expansion

In all cases, select the ones that will resonate most with the prospect, aligning them with their main evaluation criteria, business drivers, and "hot buttons."

Sales Encounters

Plan every encounter. There are many reasons for this. Whilst planning what you want to achieve and how, is the most common and valuable one, being reflective also has value, especially during a long sales and buying cycle.

Make a checklist of topics. Don't forget:

1. Why should this client see me?
2. What do I want the client to do, to advance the sale?
3. How can I provide value on this encounter?

In terms of adding value, you need to be the prospect's "trusted advisor" and domain expert, sharing with them insight and news they were not aware of, and which is unexpected.

Questions. Plan these, especially ones that add value to the prospect, because they require them to reflect, or go away and research the answer.

These questions are pivotal to a successful sales engagement.

Resist the temptation to jump in, interrupt, but instead, allow for pauses and reflection, and for others to contribute. Examples: "What do you feel will be....?," "As you reflect...," "What would you consider...."

Be very certain you know the difference between a Sales Engagement and a Sales Advancement. The most common mistaken ones include:

- The prospect asks you for a proposal.
- The prospect asks questions regarding your solution or proposal.
- You send the prospect a proposal.

None of the above are advances. That said, they are all opportunities to use to develop into advances. See Meetings Management.

Successful sales encounters, throughout the buying process, require the following:

- Emotional intelligence
- Knowledge of the customer's buying process
- Knowledge of their business

Competition

As a general principle, focus most of your energies on the client, not the competition. Most competitive offerings will be similar to yours and will also be able to deliver the same or similar outcomes.

It is therefore you, the salesperson, who will be a key factor in your success or not.

This is a very important point. You—the salesperson—make the difference.

Your main competition is as likely to be the internal competition within your prospect's organization.

There will be a limit of how many projects can happen in any one year, in terms of available budgets and more importantly, the availability of resources and staff.

Ask the prospect what other options they are considering. Some will tell you, some won't. If they are in the latter camp, then optionally challenge them by saying "some prospects choose to do so, because it helps us as suppliers draw to your attention what we believe are the differences."

Your positioning and value proposition need to reflect both the requirements of the client and who you are, or who you believe you are, competing with.

From a competition point of view, these could include factors such as: company profile, breadth of support, product maturity, number of reference clients, segment knowledge, product functions, ratio of product licenses to implementation fees, overall total cost of ownership, commercials, incumbent or new supplier, and the many aspects of risk.

Therefore, do not adopt the company standard positioning and value proposition, but amend it as necessary.

Introduce topics into the conversation if they will disadvantage the competition. You are setting the agenda, and defining a scope that suits you.

What type of company is the prospect? Are they bold adopting new ideas, new products, or leading technology? Or perhaps they have a cautious culture.

How does this affect matters between yourselves and competition?

If the firms you are competing with are not the usual "suspects" then ask yourself whether they are in the "wrong room" or are you?

Are you or your competitor an *incumbent supplier*? Perhaps they or you supply a different business in the group. Can contract terms already in place be applied to your bid? If so, this is potentially a significant advantage. Onboarding new suppliers can be onerous for both parties.

Also, the onboarding of a new supplier could be a factor if timescales for the project are aggressive.

Keep an eye out for competitors that have better senior-level contacts and relationships than you have. If third party consultancies are involved, check whether they have an existing relationship with competition, and might this put you at a disadvantage.

Your main sponsor: Have they used your competition's product before in a past life?

Is the client pretending you have competition "snapping at your heels," to keep you on your toes?

You can usually work it out based on the questions they ask, and how they answer the questions you ask them.

If you have clear advantages, then be bold and confident, but keep testing them with the client whenever you can.

How much time are you getting with the client, have they got the time and resources to run with more than one potential vendor once the evaluation process is advancing through its various stages?

Use your internal coach, if you have one, to tease out information on your competition.

Avoid complacency. No matter how much better you feel your offering is versus competition, it does not necessarily mean you will be selected.

Your main competition is often "do nothing" or an internal workaround.

And last but not least, and yes, I know you know this, but, "Never get drawn into criticising the competition."

Handling Objections

Throughout the buying process, any number of objections may be raised by the individuals involved in the evaluation of your proposition. The following are a list of tips to bear in mind when managing them.

BEST PRACTICES

Is the objection a real concern or artificial?

Is it politically motivated?

What truly lies behind the objection?

What are the implications and importance of the objection and not being able to meet it?

Address them head-on, do not be evasive.

Use the following term: "If we do xxx, will that meet your need?"

Acknowledge and avoid being dismissive of the objection, however unreasonable or illogical you feel it is.

Is it designed as a ploy for negotiating a lower price?

Set the objection in context of the overall proposition.

Objections can be a positive sign; the prospect wants them addressed so they can select you!!!

Respond to an objection with "good question, this is a topic that gets raised a lot." What this does is make the prospect feel their legitimacy, and that you have an answer to it, that others will have accepted.

If you work for a **small, early-stage supplier and you are up against an established, larger competitor**, then this may be raised as an objection. You may need to think through your positioning carefully. There are a range of factors you could potentially use to counter the objection, including:

- The importance of the differences in your offering, and their effect on business outcomes.
- If the product is early-stage, leading edge, then can the prospect afford not to adopt it, compared to a less advanced, albeit more widely established alternative?
- The many advantages of a narrow, specialist firm compared to a larger generalist.
- The means for the client to influence the direction and priorities of your product development.
- The involvement and personal commitments from senior executives.
- The ability to de-risk the project with a Proof of Concept.
- The offer of commercial concessions.
- The maturity of the product, and how proven it is.
- The strategic, business-critical nature of the proposition being considered.

PREVENTING OBJECTIONS

To avoid and minimize objections, you must build sufficient value before offering solutions.

Building sufficient value requires exploring a range of values, not just one.

If objection handling is a symptom of poor sales technique, then what is the cure? It is to learn and improve how you probe so building value is developed more effectively.

Think in terms of "Objection prevention vs objection handling."

Check that you don't apologize for anything in your offering, or introduce negatives into your conversations, even if part of your offering is not on a par with others. Why? It will trigger and feed objections.

Don't deviate away from what the client has expressed an interest in buying, by introducing other offerings, modules etc. Why? Because this can also trigger an objection, and then the tone of a meeting could change.

SUMMARY

Are you handling too many objections?

If so, it may be because you are not:

{a} Asking enough questions, and instead jumping too early into solutions, or you're not

{b} Establishing sufficient value in your offering, which will be illustrated by objections such as, "too expensive," "not worth the trouble of changing," "we're happy with our current supplier."

Proactively draw out any reservations the prospect has, so you can deal with them.

Executive Conversations

Depending on what level of seniority you typically operate at, meetings with senior executives may not be that frequent. That said, even dealing at middle management level, the topics you discuss and cover as part of a buying process should not be that different. Why?

Because any business case for change that you help develop with your sponsor will ultimately be presented up to executive level for review and approval.

Executives buy for business impact.

When meeting an executive, they will be evaluating what you have to say and the potential value of your proposition in the context of the following:

- Macroeconomic and external pressures from the market, the economy, etc
- Their own internal business programs
- The level of disruption your proposition would have on their organization (this can be both operationally and culturally)
- The financials, and potential return on investment
- Risk factors

- Personal factors (can they visualize being a hero, doing interviews, enhancing their desire for promotion)

They will typically respond positively to items such as:
- Research / trends from their industry
- Benchmarks on how they compare to their peer organizations
- Unconsidered needs
- Insight about their customers
- Opportunities to meet their peers
- Statistics to support any claims you make
- Reference clients and case studies, with business outcomes that were achieved
- How you mitigate risks and avoid unnecessary disruption when implementing your offering
- A proposition that enables the business to be better managed

Some of the above items may be sensitive: for example, if it is widely known that this prospect performs poorly in a certain area.

You may choose to adopt a particular strategy in terms of what messaging you use. Four popular and proven ones are:

Unique Value Proposition: your offering will address their need "better" than alternatives.

Known Initiative: you know there is an initiative underway, you can address the needs, and the ROI is xx, based on proven case studies.

Provocative / Sensitive Industry Insight: as illustrated above.

Competitive Benchmarks: as above.

Recent studies show that the latter two have a much better impact on securing a meeting.

The "Data, Insight, Question" approach can effectively support this type of approach too.

Access to a senior executive will often be through an internal champion or sponsor they trust, with whom you have been dealing. Ensure you are thoroughly briefed on hot-button topics, and topics to avoid.

Gaining access to a senior executive can be challenging. Your chances are improved depending on how you look and how you sound; they need to perceive you as a peer. You need confidence, competence (in your subject) and a compelling reason why they should see you.

That said, you, or a senior executive from your organization, cannot afford not to meet them; they will be more influential in the decision making than you may think, and your competitors will probably be meeting them.

Senior executives will rarely delegate risk.

Don't forget, your biggest enemy will be "do nothing" and remaining with the status quo. So you need to address the "Why Now?" question.

Be respectful but be confident of what you can bring to the meeting that will be of value.

Here's some research from Forrester, so you know what is at stake:

- Eighty-six percent (86%) of salespeople calling on an executive failed to have an intelligent conversation.
- The first person to paint a plausible vision for the future has a 74% chance of closing a deal.

Therefore, you need to identify the gap between an organization's current situation and their business vision.

Read the chairman's foreword in the recent accounts, or search on the internet for interviews with senior executives, and investor presentations.

Always be on the lookout for a catalyst to use, to create interest and momentum. These can either be external or internal factors.

You are endeavoring to be seen as a trusted advisor, so align your knowledge with context unique to the executive and their organization.

Prepare, and do so thoroughly. If at all possible, find out how the executive is measured in their job.

Align your proposal to important areas to show how it can improve them. Typical examples include:

- Cost controls
- Operating margin
- Revenue
- Cash flow
- Customer service
- Reputational risk

An economic justification will be a mix of hard, soft, and strategic benefits.

Demonstrate as early as you can during the opening that you have prepared and researched beforehand. The executive needs to know as quickly as possible they are meeting with a professional who will not waste their time.

Prepare a proposed next step.

Prepare a reason for you to remain in touch with the executive, so your access remains open as the buying process develops.

Do Nothing: The Barriers

Anywhere from 60–80% of initiatives result in the status quo remaining and the prospect "doing nothing" with you or any other supplier. There can be many reasons, some you will have some control over, and some you won't.

However, what is absolutely key is you try and tease out the likelihood of this happening as early in the sales process as possible to avoid wasting time.

Here are some of the signs to look out for and assess, to get a feel for the likelihood the client will end up not making a decision (or not selecting your offer):

- You are always chasing them for follow-ups
- Internal inertia
- Budgets
- The project will impose too much disruption on current internal systems or processes
- Availability of resources
- Other more pressing priorities
- Not compelling enough to change
- Cultural mismatches

- Little or no buy-in from the users of the system / product
- Perception of risk
- Your risk as a supplier
- Something similar was tried before, and results were disappointing, or a "do nothing" decision was made
- A stakeholder has a personal investment / reputation to protect the status quo
- Industry failures of something similar
- Careers are at stake, and your internal sponsor does not have the personality to pursue this
- Timing of the engagement
- The proposal fails to deliver the necessary return on investment
- No compelling event, it is more a "nice to have"
- Doesn't align with an individual's performance criteria of how they are judged
- Company ethos: early adopter, fast follower, or laggard
- Is or isn't part of a larger program that is dictating timescales and priorities
- Your internal sponsor holds little influence with decision makers / budget holders

"*Change is Constant*," so look out for events such as:
- The company reorganizes, decision makers change roles, or they lose influence
- There is a merger or acquisition announcement

- There is a change in business strategy
- The company's operating performance deteriorates
- There is a significant external event

That said, be on the lookout for a trigger event, to load the arguments <u>against</u> "do nothing."

- Use research, industry trends and best practices to drive the message "you need to change"
- A change in legislation
- A successful project announcement from a competitor
- Can the prospect realistically (continue) to do nothing; have they fallen asleep at the wheel? How do they compare with their peers? Can they afford for this to continue? What will the consequences be?

When you show a vision to the future, the likelihood of engagement increases.

The decision of a company whether to Do Nothing will be influenced by the risk of doing it or not doing it, the effort involved, and the value of the outcome. These need to be aligned in your favor and underpin your value proposition.

Continuously tease out possible reasons for "doing nothing," so that those you can overcome are addressed to the satisfaction of the prospect. If they are left to fester, they will be more difficult to overcome at a later stage.

Which is why regular communication with the prospect is crucial.

As stated in other Sections, your role is pivotal throughout the buying process. The more support you provide your sponsor, the more likely they will want to construct a compelling business case for the business sponsors to approve.

Furthermore, it is your role to provide your sponsor with the materials, arguments, and evidence they can use internally with their stakeholders.

Negotiations

Depending upon your role and frequency of deals, you may only formally negotiate contract and commercials infrequently, therefore an aide memoire of the key principles is valuable.

While you may be negotiating with a large, well-resourced organization, do not assume the person you negotiate with is trained and highly skilled in doing so.

Pricing: To achieve a "win/win" for both parties, it ideally requires a commercial proposal that has been priced and structured in such a way that you have built-in meaningful concessions you can offer, while protecting overall profit margins.

Preparation: The relative complexity of the sales cycle, value of the contract, and contract terms will determine the depth of preparation you do. The minimum preparation are the "red line" terms, the upper and lower limit of the commercials, the opening offer you make, the concession strategy you adopt, the concession items available to you, and the concessions you want in return.

Don't be the first to concede, and do not make concessions too early. When you do offer a concession, then the first one needs to be meaningful, but any further ones are incrementally smaller.

Know which items are available to you as "empty" concessions (they don't cost you anything but have value to the customer).

Knowing the price of something does not mean you know the "value" of it.

Thoroughly think through and anticipate what the customer wants out of the negotiation, and will value highly.

Effective negotiations need trust. One method is called mirroring and labelling. Mirroring is using terms and words back in your negotiations that your counterpart is using. Labelling is acknowledging the person's feelings or position.

If you hear a "ly" word, then that is a signal there is "wiggle room." Words such as "usually, typically, normally."

The use of the word "decided," will mean that there was an alternative decision under consideration, and gives you an opportunity to explain "why" you are the exception.

Who will be signing off on the deal? Addressing these stakeholders' needs and "win results" needs to be a key focus.

Don't settle and agree on a price without ensuring all requirements have been captured. Using terms such as the following is very effective:

"I fully appreciate price is important to you, but before addressing that, I'd like to take a moment to make sure I fully understand your needs, so we can make sure we do everything we can to provide you the best overall value."

If the terms change, the price changes. This means items such as adding in functions or modules, extending the scope, or reducing the timescales.

If a discount is requested, ask why. Using terms such as, "What are you looking to achieve with a 20% price reduction?" rather than, "I can give you 10% but I can't do 20%."

The majority of people assign more value to "avoiding the risk of a loss," rather than the opportunity to "make a gain."

If you cannot or do not want to agree or offer a concession, explain why not. (this gives it more substance and is less likely to be challenged / insisted upon)

Do not fall into the trap of getting drawn into negotiating with your main point of contact until you know whether he or she is the final negotiator. To avoid offending this person, you can inquire what the procurement and approval process is, and the role of each of those that will be involved and responsible for reviewing and approving the contract.

What is your assessment of your power, and their perception of this? And vice versa, what is your perception of their power and how they perceive it?

Set yourself high targets and expectations.

Manage information skillfully, because information is power and provides leverage.

Focus on customer needs, to enable value to be drawn out and negotiated.

Anticipate difficult questions.

Prioritize your concession items, in accordance with your concession strategy.

Both sides need to feel they are winning as the negotiation progresses, and of course at the end when it concludes.

Talk is cheap, don't allow yourself to be talked into something without being convinced they will "walk the walk."

Do not negotiate over email. If there are a couple of terms that need to be negotiated, then in an email suggest, "Let's jump on a call; should only need a few minutes."

Closing

Do not use gambits; these techniques are crass, will damage trust, and will be counterproductive. BUT you have to initiate a closing process.

A major sale will not close itself. You must make an effort to advance or close the sale.

Overcoming the **psychology of Closing**:

"You are not selling, the customer is buying, and you are providing a Service."

Your language and manner should be natural, and no different to what went before.

A good Closing Approach needs to be:

- At the customer's pace (within reason)
- Accommodating
- Not problematic for the customer

Which is why "traditional closing gambits" do not work and should not be used.

The client needs to feel they are in control, while you are coaching them as necessary.

Trust accelerates sales.

While you may not have the above luxury if operating under pressure with a quarter-end or annual target to meet, the above should always be followed in the first case.

The knack of course is to manage and pace the sales and buying process, such that the closing process aligns with your target dates.

What is closing? A firm commitment to buy.

Psychologically, making a client aware that they are closer to their goal than they may have realized, and letting them know how much progress has been made, will actually accelerate their efforts toward closure.

Frequent and consistent Advances facilitate the Closing of a deal. These are incremental steps that move the process closer to a decision.

Every day the deal does not close, the opportunity is at risk. Maintain momentum. Agree "by when" the next task will be completed.

The price is usually one of the first topics that gets negotiated. Anchoring a price is an effective technique for both buyer and seller to use, to set the expectations for the other side: what they are looking for from the deal.

This anchoring of price may happen during formal negotiations or earlier in the buying process.

As a salesperson, let's say you are targeting a price of $100,000, then you may say: "The published price that our clients pay for this model is $115,000. With add-ons, some pay as much as $125,000. However, I know you won't be using all of the features, so on that basis, I am willing to agree a slightly lower price." You have anchored between $115,000 and $125,000, but indicated you are willing to agree slightly less.

Mind you, watch out for the buyer using the same technique on you!!

Communication

Whether written or verbal, the use of language is crucially important. To avoid making the job of sales any more difficult than it needs to be, follow these tips.

Avoid "wishy-washy" words such as: "think" (either something needs to happen or it doesn't), "just" (avoid this like the plague), "guess" (replace with estimate, forecast, expectation), "need," and "very, highly, extremely."

Pandering: avoid phrases such as, "I'd be glad to meet you, at your convenience, we're pleased to..."

The above reduces your credibility; clients want to work with their peers in the industry, which is how you should project yourself.

If you don't believe in what you are saying or communicating, it will show through to others.

If one word can convey what five words convey, then use one word. Keep communication as short as possible.

Condensing your big idea into 50 or **fewer words** will make your pitch stronger, easier to remember, and ultimately more likely that your listener will act on the idea.

Use the word "you," and make the recipient the hero / center of the story.

PEOPLE CHARACTERISTICS

Their hobbies provide an insight into their personality. Personality is made up of four components:

- *Energy*—extrovert/introvert
- *Information* they pay attention to—sensor / intuition
- How they make *decisions*—think or feel
- How they *organize* their world—judgers / perceivers

DEALING EFFECTIVELY WITH PEOPLE

- "I can see that," is a **visual** person who will need to see things.
- "I hear what you are saying," is an **auditory** person who will be okay to talk to on the phone.
- "I can't get to grips with this," is **kinaesthetic** and will respond best to a hands-on demo.

NEURO-LINGUISTIC PROGRAMMING (NLP)

The basis of this concept is mirroring the mannerisms the person on the other side of the desk is using. This is an effective way of improving how you engage with someone.

Research suggests good communication is 7% words, 38% tone, 55% body language.

Tell **stories**: they maximise impact in all communication.

Personality types: Based upon Myers-Briggs research, four types of buyers were identified:

Pragmatists, drivers, commanders: Motivated by facts (though not too many), quick to decide, especially if they can see a bottom-line affect.

Analytical people: Require detailed presentations. Slower to decide. Need lots of information. They must be pushed.

Expressive people or visionaries: Quick to act and respond based upon emotional insights. Big-picture people. Less interested in your product versus whether it will help them achieve their own ideas and goals.

Amiable, consensus seekers: Tend to value close working relationships. Get confused or intimidated by a lot of technical detail but do respond to the personal touch.

Your client may not like you taking **comprehensive notes**, it feels like a deposition, and too little like having a conversation. Limit it as much as possible.

You will be surprised how much you can retrieve from your memory, by noting a one-or two-word trigger.

WE MAKE DECISIONS BASED ON THREE THINGS

- *Reflexive*, based on experience, (the theory underpinning the top selling book *Thinking Fast and Slow*, by Daniel Kahneman)
- *Habit,* because it worked in the past, or
- Decisions driven by *targets*.

Leverage these when communicating.

Dale Carnegie wrote and spoke about **the power of enthusiasm**; namely that enthusiasm is contagious.

He suggests six ways to make people like you:

- Be genuinely interested in them.
- Smile.
- Remember that a man's / woman's name is the sweetest and most important sound in any language.
- Be a good listener, encourage others to talk about themselves.
- Talk in terms of the other person's interest.
- Make the other person feel important; do it sincerely.

Make facts and messages, vivid, interesting, and dramatic. Use showmanship. Use anecdotes. Tell stories.

Because people love to talk about themselves, ask questions that create emotions.

The Carnegie approach, is based upon listening, showing sincere appreciation, and an interest in them.

As stated above, the NLP approach involves techniques called "mirroring" and "pacing."

Mirroring involves mimicking the other person's speech patterns, tone of voice, diction, body language, facial expressions, and other outward expressions of the person's "meta-style."

Ban "how are you?" from your lexicon of terms.

Recent research concluded the following steps improve communication:

Don't say "talk," use "speak."

Also replace the word "anything" with "something."

For example, "is there anything else / something else you wanted to discuss?"

BE CLEAR AND CONCISE

- **S**tart by thinking, not talking.
- **H**ome in on the main idea quickly.
- **A**dd details sparingly.
- **R**elate to the audience.
- **P**repare.

You can successfully communicate ideas by doing the following, as presented by physicist Dominic Walliman in a Ted Talk:

- Start off at the right place in terms of where your audience is.
- Don't lose the plot, stay on track, and don't get dragged down a rabbit hole.
- Focus on clarity over accuracy: cover the details and nuances once the core principles are understood.
- Be enthusiastic.

WRITTEN COMMUNICATION

Detail people want information, ideas people want concepts.

Avoid words like: Best of breed, world class, quality focused, uniquely qualified, high performance, synergy, user friendly, integrated, partnership, seamless, robust.

Using legal terms in an email suggests you don't trust the reader. So why should they trust you?

Tone is difficult to teach yet is critically important. Keep a watchful eye on the tone of your communication.

One discipline that helps with both clear communication and time management when dealing with a high volume of emails is the five-sentence principle: When responding to an email, whatever the context, always keep it to five sentences. Try it; you will be surprised how effective this is.

Never communicate when you are **emotional**, particularly by email. Also remember that emails and messaging cannot capture the nuance of language, so be careful.

Place the important content in the body of a document / proposal, and all supplementary and supporting information in an appendix.

Will I Hit Target?

Have you **realistically** got long enough to close the deals before the end of the target period? Are you over-reliant on a small number of opportunities?

Has someone else in your organization evaluated and critiqued your pipeline and the deals you are depending on? For example, your sales leader?

By end of Q2, if sales cycles are up to six months, what ratio of the pipeline are qualified opportunities?

3 x target is minimum for most situations.

Your pipeline needs continual, objective monitoring and evaluating, preferably with someone else. Search for both positive and negative trends.

Are you looking through rose-tinted glasses?

Look at all the things that could go wrong and build in compensating tactics to minimize the probability of them happening.

Momentum is key; without it, the probability of a deal in the timescales you are forecasting is seriously affected.

Focus on the Critical Success Factors of each deal.

If a deal falls away, can you replace it with something else?

Can you potentially increase the proposal value of an existing deal to offset against the potential for lost deals or deals that close at a lower value than expected?

Have you asked your point of contact whether your timescales are aligned with theirs, and are realistic?

Do they have a compelling event aligned with your timescales?

Are you over-reliant on something that is not under your control? For example: a new release of your software, or an ongoing project inside your prospect that needs to finish first.

Use techniques to align their timescales with yours. For example, promise to make a certain implementation team available to their project if the deal closes by the end of the quarter / year. (Use this sparingly.)

The Mental Side of Sales

To be read in conjunction with other Sections, especially Prospecting.

Sales, especially new business sales, can be dispiriting at times, so the mental side of the job is important.

It can also be a lonely place.

Maintaining motivation is not always easy.

When push comes to shove, people only do what they truly want to do.

The drive and pressure to hit the sales target will sustain most salespeople for a while.

But if you haven't yet figured out exactly what you want and why you want it, you will find motivation more difficult over the long term and during particularly challenging periods.

Maintaining motivation aligns with both internal and external factors. The former relates to your core principles, beliefs and standards, the latter to necessities like paying the mortgage, and supporting your family.

Finally, picking up that phone when you have had a day of voicemails and rejections (a bit of an old school example, but you know what I mean), is easier if you genuinely believe in what you are doing and why.

You are not selling. You are serving and servicing your customers and prospects. You are helping them to be heroes and meet their business goals. You are not a pest.

That said, if you feel you are not in the right frame of mind for a particular task, such as Prospecting, then do something else.

If you're struggling with negative self-talk:

- Write down a list of positive things about you and why people need what you offer, and
- Every time you have a negative thought, read at least three of these things back to yourself.

When approaching a call or a meeting, don't go in with an expectation of what is reasonable, go in with an objective of what is possible.

Employ positive thinking. Expect to win / achieve the "unexpected." After all, you have no idea the situation or context in which the prospect finds his or herself.

The prospect may have been assigned a task to resolve something that your product is designed for, earlier that week.

You may be in the right place at the right time.

A mindset such as this will improve the likelihood of positive outcomes.

Set expectations as high as possible, a "stretch," but realistic.

Visualize positive outcomes to sales encounters.

Don't be hard on yourself if things are not going your way. Every salesperson suffers from self-doubt at one time or another. They just hide it.

That said, if you keep being disappointed, you need to evaluate what you are doing, how it can be improved, and whether something needs to change.

Some prospects may seem intimidating to deal with; they may be doing this consciously or subconsciously. Be aware of how you react to this and deal with it. Don't allow it to unnerve you.

If you are working at home a great deal more than you were pre-Covid 19 pandemic, make sure your work environment is conducive to quality work.

For some people, how they dress can and does affect the quality of their work and attitudes. You may be one of them.

Develop friendships and contacts that are good for you mentally and spiritually. Mentors can be good too.

A problem shared is a problem halved.

Sales is never a nine-to-five job and can be a highly pressurized environment, especially when under pressure to hit sales targets. So keep an eye on burnout. Take regular breaks. Get plenty of fresh air and exercise.

Miscellaneous Tips & Thoughts

The following is a range of thoughts and tips collected over time that have proved useful.

No Regrets: Be bold in life and when appropriate, take a risk. Generally speaking, people regret things that they didn't do rather than what they did.

Do Not Assume: It's a golden oldie, but don't forget it!

Don't Judge Me: "Unless you have walked a mile in my shoes, don't judge me." Another well-known saying, and one that has great merit in sales when dealing with many different people.

B2B SALES IS A PROFESSION

Just consider for a moment the skills you need to learn and continually develop to perform the role. Communication skills, both verbal and written, knowledge of financials, working with numbers, legal contract knowledge, the ability to work under pressure, negotiations, working in a team, leadership, managing people, knowing how to deal with a wide range of types of people in a client organization and your own, knowledge of marketing, proficiency with desktop applications, business knowledge of the sector you are operating in, knowledge of what you are selling, and last but not least, selling.

TAKING NOTES

Develop a technique for taking as few notes as possible in a meeting while still capturing the core points. Why? The less notes you take, the more engaged you can be with your customer.

Furthermore, it is off-putting to have someone take down almost word for word what you say.

Draw a line down the middle of the page. On the left side head it Capture and on the right side title it Create.

Under Capture, record in bullet points the facts you wish to remember and recall.

Down the right-hand side (Create) record when you have an idea or emotion triggered by what the other person has said; ideas like how, why, and when you might use what has just been said.

Emotions also help the recall of facts.

QUESTIONING

When something goes wrong, instead of getting angry or disappointed and attempting to fix it, why not question why it went wrong? You will improve many aspects of your life adopting this approach, and improve your overall sales performance.

HUMAN BEINGS ARE NOT RATIONAL BEINGS

This is the underlying premise of the book by Daniel Kahneman, *Thinking, Fast and Slow*. The decisions we make are influenced by a great many things, many of which do not logically make sense. To be able to deal with this in sales, and navigate a long complex buying cycle involving many different individuals, train yourself to question why someone behaves the way they do, rather than react to what they have done or said.

INNOVATION: THE GOOGLE 20% RULE

Google employees are encouraged to spend 20% of their working week exploring ideas that are speculative with no likelihood of immediate return. Why not try this idea? You may be surprised by the ideas you get. That said, 20% sounds too high to spend.

TIME MANAGEMENT

Preparing for an important meeting or creating a presentation? Assign an amount of time and stick to it. Better still, assign less time than usual, so you are under pressure.

Focus on your desired objective and outcome for the meeting, and ensure these are the main criteria that influence the amount of time you give yourself to prepare for it.

What you produce will probably not be materially different. The overall outcomes of the meeting are unlikely to be affected by spending more time than is necessary, so discipline yourself not to do so.

Most brains are at their best first thing in the morning, so use this time for substantial tasks like writing a proposal, rather than reviewing emails or updating an internal MIS system.

Keep working on the discipline required to avoid being distracted by the constant communication of emails, social media updates, etc. Carve out sections of the day for them, and stick to the schedule.

Find time to think. Don't just have an endless list of to dos.

AWAY ON VACATION?

Want to avoid an enormous inbox of emails when you get back? On your Out of Office message, write: "I am away for 2 weeks from Monday xx. During this time I will not be reading emails, and when I return, I will only attend to emails received from the day I return to work."

BUILDING RELATIONSHIPS

People love to talk about themselves. Select topics and ask questions that trigger emotions. Be genuinely interested.

Remember what they said last time you met.

Ask questions that make the other person pause and reflect.

Avoid closed questions.

People buy from people. Building a relationship with your prospect is key. Never, ever forget this.

BUILDING A NETWORK OF CONTACTS THROUGHOUT YOUR CAREER

I have neglected this compared to many of my peers, and it is something I regret. While it wasn't easy until LinkedIn launched, on hindsight, I wish I had done more. That said, I am a great believer in quality over quantity. I rarely Connect with anyone unless I have met them in person or virtually, or at least had a meaningful interaction with them. The criterion I apply is: if someone in my network approaches me with a request to be introduced to someone I am Connected to, at a minimum I want to be able to do so, and be able to explain the context in which I know them.

SELF-LEARNING

I have maintained a career in sales for over thirty years. When you consider the industry I operate in, namely technology sales of high-value software and services to the banking segment, and the dramatic changes that have taken place during that time, this is no mean feat.

Many of my peers over the years fell by the wayside. One of the reasons for this is they became less effective because their skills and approach failed to adapt to change. I didn't, however. I put this down to the initiatives I took, and continue to take, in self-learning. I have never relied on my employers to provide this, but have proactively gone out and searched for it myself. Hence this book includes a vast range of information drawn from a wide set of sources over a lifetime in sales.

MENTORS

If you are relatively early in your sales career, keep an eye out for a mentor, and when you find one, adopt them. Either by formally asking them, or allowing the relationship to develop naturally. If you are more experienced, then actively encourage less experienced salespeople to adopt you as a mentor. It is both deeply satisfying and a valuable means to check that the advice you are giving, you are actually following yourself!

STARTING A NEW JOB

The honeymoon period you enjoy when you are new in a job will not last long. The expectations of management may not match reality, so you need to set theirs aligned with reality while not projecting a negative, unambitious attitude. This is not always easy, especially if you are inheriting a sales pipeline that the previous salesperson presented as more advanced that it was.

What I do in these circumstances is write my sales plan, including the first 100 days, with key deliverables. I present this to my management, and get their comments and agreement. Both parties are now invested in the plan. While you execute against the plan, make sure you continually communicate your progress, and share with them any challenges or obstacles. The communication piece is absolutely key; do not allow it to fall by the wayside. The trust you build up by communicating and getting their buy-in is crucial.

PROBLEM SOLVING

From time to time we are faced with solving a problem involving a moral or ethical dilemma. As a salesperson, it may involve the ethics about promises you make to a client, for example. Research shows that most companies and people frame the problem in terms of "What should we do?" But this limits the options. However, if you reframe the question to "What could we do?" then this simple change of word seems to result in more choices and better solutions. Perhaps try it for yourself.

SALES UNPLUGGED: PART 2
STORIES FROM THE FRONT LINE

THE TIMES THEY ARE A-CHANGIN': BOB DYLAN

My sales career began in 1987. If you are a Millennial or Gen-Z, this must seem like the dark ages. That year, major film releases included *Platoon*, *Fatal Attraction*, *RoboCop*, and the first *Lethal Weapon*. Michael Jackson released *Bad*.

Personal computers were only just beginning to penetrate the workplace, but very few could be found in the home. PCs had 5 ¼ inch floppy disks and monitors that weighed a ton. Windows had only just been released, while before that, it had been MS DOS. I still use Ctrl C, Ctrl V, and Ctrl X on my keyboard for copy, paste and cut.

Smoking was just being banned on the London Underground, and fax was the main method of communication between businesses; email didn't establish itself until the early 1990s.

The company I was working for at the time also had a telex room we could use when we needed to.

My first sales role was in a major account team; in this case Barclays Bank. I was working for NCR, previously known as The National Cash Register Company. (How old-fashioned a name does that sound?!)

NCR at the time was dominant in the through-the-wall cash dispensing machines, check processing systems, Point of Sale terminals, and retail supermarket checkouts.

The company also had a long history of manufacturing mainframes, which had to be housed in air conditioned computer rooms. The processing power of a mainframe in those days was less than the equivalent of what we carry around in our pockets today.

My first role in sales involved submitting proposals, typically in response to a formal RFP. We hand-wrote them, and gave them to the office manager or secretary to type. For substantial pieces of work, we could use the typing pool.

Our account team had our own stationary cupboard, with preprinted stationary, with the Barclays logo in the header.

Print jams, and running out of the pre-printed paper, were a constant cause of frustration. We also had to factor in the number of copies we needed. It was always a minimum of five, and could go up to a dozen. These were for distributing to the various stakeholders involved in the bid at the bank.

When you consider the proposals were sometimes over a hundred pages, we needed boxes to pack the proposals into, a glossy front cover, and a courier on standby to transport the proposals overnight for delivery by the deadline the following morning.

Occasionally, if we failed to hit the deadline by 6 p.m., (couriers did not pick up and collect later than this), then one of us would have to drive it up the motorway 200 miles at five in the morning to deliver it by hand. I am not joking.

I won't even share with you the challenge of sprocket punching, collating the proposals by hand, discovering a page missing after the print room had shut, and bindings that were not strong enough for the size of the proposal!

Makes you properly appreciate email, attachments, and the cc function!!

As the 1980s gave way to the 1990s, email and mobile phones were introduced. Both slowly transformed business, but would still look archaic by today's standards.

And don't forget, Tim Berners Lee didn't invent the World Wide Web until 1989. And throughout the 1990s, gaining access to it was a fraught process of modem dial-ups, incompatible routers, network bandwidth measured in kilobytes, and so on.

In 1994, I moved from NCR to a small company, located a two and a half hour drive from where I lived. So I was an early pioneer of working from home, visiting the office only once a week.

That said, it was challenging, especially the need to be self-sufficient, with no secretary or office manager to call upon. Faxes and dialing up the modem were the bane of my life.

Client meetings and presentations were the best. Because there was no PowerPoint, we used acetates, which we either hand wrote using colored felt-tip pens or printed them by loading the photocopier up with the acetates. Printer jams were common.

In sales, end of year and end of quarter were much like they are today. Stressful. The difference then, however, was how slow communications were for written confirmations.

Remarkably, when a customer couldn't get the necessary order through their internal processes, we would plead for them to send us a Letter of Intent. This expressed their intention to purchase a certain set of goods and services at a given price. The letter was not legally binding, but it was sometimes enough to get a deal booked if we made a strong enough case to the Sales Director. And we are not talking minor deals. I remember a $10 million plus deal was approved for hundreds of ATMs using the LOI.

I could go on.

While all of the above technology examples were general, and applied to everyone, my sales career has involved and rubbed shoulders with some pioneering innovations.

Do you take for granted that you can access a local government website, and be able to view the details of a planning application with detailed drawings? Well, in 1995 I was working for a document management and workflow software company that pioneered this, and implemented what I think was the first project providing this service in the UK. It was at the London Borough of Wandsworth.

I remember that I was deeply skeptical for a number of reasons.

The first was because it was going to cost the local authority money to set it up and launch the service, yet they knew they would not be able to charge the public to use the service. This seemed a ridiculous concept at the time.

Furthermore, only 27% of householders in the UK owned a computer, many of which did not have access to the internet, as it was still very much in its infancy. The networks were slow too, especially for scanned documents such as planning applications.

I was also dubious because a product manager in our company was leading the initiative and working with the customer, not a salesperson.

However, both Phil, the product manager, and the guy at the council had vision, unlike me. Together, they were convinced of its merit, and the future of the internet, and how it could serve the public.

And of course, they were proven right, and I was proven wrong.

It was a salient lesson.

Since then I have learned to be more open minded to new ideas, and recognize how quickly society can change its habits and expectations as technology advances at an ever-quickening pace. The metaverse is a current example.

Prior to this, while at NCR I specialized in check processing systems. This was at the time when hand-written checks were still a prominent means of payment, alongside cash and the emerging credit and debit cards.

The innovation I saw close up and helped promote was applying optical-based character recognition software to the hand-written amount on the checks.

With this innovation, the checks could be loaded into a hopper and processed automatically without manually keying the amounts. The potential savings for the banks were huge.

The very largest ones had regional centers with hundreds of data processing clerks manually keying the checks, day in, day out.

Being at the "bleeding-edge" of this technology was challenging, stressful, and full of highs and lows. These included managing customer demonstrations, meeting deadlines, rushing out new releases of the software that turned out to be full of bugs and errors, and dealing with a development center six time zones away in Dayton Ohio.

It required highly tuned sales techniques to prevent the customer losing faith, and feeling it was too much a risk to go ahead.

The point I am making is that throughout my career, I have needed to adapt and embrace new technology, the emergence of new business practices, and societal changes. I did so reluctantly and hesitantly during the early days, but now of course adapt to them more readily.

That said, a few months ago, I was clearing out some cupboards, and came upon some old sales training manuals. Although some practices have surprisingly stood the test of time quite well, some are truly archaic and irrelevant.

While my sales career has coincided with arguably the most extraordinary era of technological innovation, and societal dynamics the world has seen, it will continue for the foreseeable future. AI, ChatGPT, the metaverse, brain implants, robotics, space exploration, climate change, cyberattacks, facial recognition, and social media will all in their own way impact the role of sales, so the need to adapt and embrace them to sustain a long career will remain crucial.

That said, if you operate in business to business selling, and what you are selling is not a commodity and involves a level of salesperson involvement, then building relationships, being trustworthy, and fulfilling the role of a trusted advisor will still outweigh everything else.

WHO ARE YOU?: THE WHO

"**O**y, Grant-y, what you doin'?" I looked around, but needn't have done so. I recognized the gruff, slurred cockney voice immediately. It was the VP of sales of the banking division in the UK.

It's 1987. I was walking towards the office one afternoon. I had only recently moved into a sales role from a sales support job. I had already begun adopting my style and image, namely a suit, a colored button-down shirt, matching tie, handkerchief, and socks. The socks would often be white, red, or yellow.

His appointment a few months prior to this had taken everyone by surprise. It wasn't that he wasn't a successful salesman who consistently met and exceeded targets, because he was. It's just that he was uncouth, rude, scruffily dressed, and badly spoken. This was not the typical profile of a sales manager at NCR, especially in the sedate world of banking and computer systems.

"On my way to Headquarters, Bill. I have a meeting with the Product Team."

"Oh yeah, well you don't want to be spending too much time with them you know. You're in sales now. You need to change your ways. Also, it's not a fashion show, you need to dress more appropriately. Get rid of them white socks." He hiccupped and stumbled up close to me, unable to walk a straight line. His breath stank of beer.

"Also, I'll give you another piece of advice. You were born with two ears and one mouth for a reason. So don't forget it."

And at that point, he stumbled off towards the office, while I purposely slowed down, to delay my arrival time.

While the manner in which the advice was delivered left a great deal to be desired, the advice itself was spot on.

I later reflected on what he had said.

The first point I didn't like. I felt different than a great number of the salespeople in the banking division. I looked upon them as staid and conservative, while I was hip. I played in a rock band, wore my hair longer than most, wore fashionable clothes, and had recently had a book published. So I wanted to stand out and liked the style I had adopted. But he had made a good point. The colored socks did look a bit twee, especially when I wore white. That was not a professional business look.

The second piece of advice was excellent and I embraced it immediately. It was not difficult. A great many people were shocked when I said I was moving into a sales job. I am not and was not an extrovert, so listening and not talking came naturally. It is one of my strengths, and one of the main qualities that have enabled me to enjoy a relatively long, successful career. I don't have a huge ego, so I don't mind others taking center stage.

So why share this anecdote with you?

The point is that there is no blueprint for a successful and effective salesperson that consistently hits their sales target.

They can be male, female, tall, short, fat, thin, scruffy, smart, introvert, extrovert, outspoken, unassuming, young, old, and so on.

But be true to yourself and your family.

You need to be able to look yourself in the mirror each morning and be proud of what you see.

If you've got what it takes, it will shine through. After all, cream always floats to the top!

That said, if this means going out on a limb, then you need to do so.

I have been vegetarian since the mid-1980s.

At the time, this caused me a great deal of internal strife.

One of the first lessons I learned in sales and believe in fully is that when you invite a client out to lunch or dinner, their needs will be first and foremost. You want them to relax and have a nice time.

You certainly don't want them to ever feel uncomfortable.

If the service is poor or my meal is not hot, for example, I think very carefully before complaining, for fear of embarrassing my guest.

You will no doubt apply more modern equivalents that you face both today and in the years ahead, such as the Metaverse.

PLANES, TRAINS & AUTOMOBILES: 1987 MOVIE STARRING STEVE MARTIN AND JOHN CANDY

In September 2015, I experienced one of the most hectic, demanding, and exhilarating weeks of my business life that I can recall.

At the time I was working for an Austrian software company with headquarters in the delightful city of Vienna. If you've not been, and you ever get the opportunity to visit, make sure you visit one of the classic coffee houses. The sheer elegance and sense of tradition are intoxicating; the cakes and pastries are great too, especially the apple strudel.

However, I digress.

At the time I was country manager in the UK.

This tale began on a Monday, with a visit to headquarters. It was a flying visit, requiring a 5:00 a.m. alarm call to catch the first flight out of Heathrow, and a return home the same day at 10:00 in the evening. I was finalizing the details and planning for an event later that week, in Copenhagen.

I spent Tuesday in London, and on Wednesday flew the three hours to Copenhagen in time for registration at midday.

The timing of the conference coincided with a major bid I was involved in with the sovereign wealth fund of Abu Dhabi. This was time-consuming but stimulating. The size and scope of the deal were the largest and most complex the company had ever undertaken. Dealing with the differences in culture and business protocols, and the distance between us in Europe and them in the Middle East, further contributed to the challenge.

While at the conference, I received a surprising email. It was notification that they were planning a visit to Europe the following week, and would like to visit us Monday in Vienna, to finalize contract negotiations.

They apologized for the short notice, but requested that our best and final bid be submitted by end of business Friday, so they could review it on the Sunday prior to the meeting.

The remainder of the conference was a whirlwind of meetings, emails, and late-night spreadsheets. The bid ran into many millions of dollars, uncharted territory for us at the time. It also involved software modules that were incomplete and still under development. The complexity of the bid was exacerbated by the need for us to factor in months and months of travelling expenses, and staff being away from home.

I remember our biggest concern was avoiding "sticker shock." While they had already received from us a range of commercials, putting them all together into a single bid that would be contractually binding highlighted how many millions they would need to invest for the project to proceed to the scope they were requesting. We weren't sure they had the necessary budget and business case to support it.

However, before leaving the conference on Friday to fly back, we had somehow managed to agree among ourselves on the details of the final bid; it just needed me to proofread it on the plane, and email it to the client when I got home.

As I sat on the tube from London's Heathrow at 10 p.m., I knew I was still facing a great many tasks when I eventually arrived home.

That weekend I was booked to go on a cycling trip to Cambridge with a group of guys. About fifty miles of cycling, and a return the following day. So I would need to pack for that.

In addition to issuing the proposal to the client, I needed to plan my visit to Vienna. So I needed a flight on Sunday evening, returning on Monday evening, and an overnight hotel stay.

I needed to be back that Monday evening in London because I had a 7:00 a.m. hospital appointment on Tuesday for an operation to remove a cyst from my jaw.

I finally got to bed about one in the morning and was up again in time to cycle the thirty minutes or so to the designated spot for an 8 o'clock meet.

The cycling up to Cambridge and back was, thank goodness, without incident. That said, cycling the morning after a long night out with eight other guys on a "boys weekend away" was not ideal.

By lunch time Sunday, we were about ten miles from home. I abandoned the guys to their pub lunch and cycled the remainder on my own. Within ninety minutes of arriving home, I was showered, changed, packed with suit in hand, and on the tube back to Heathrow. There had been little room for error.

The negotiations went ahead as planned on Monday, and I left the meeting at 5:30 to get the 8 p.m. flight back to Heathrow, home at midnight, and up again before 6 to get down to the hospital for 7.

I have never had a week like that before or since.

That said, it was all worthwhile. We signed contracts with the client by the end of the year, and the operation on my jaw went smoothly, albeit not without a great deal of pain and discomfort.

The experience reminded me that when push comes to shove, and you are working under pressure, there is a need for resilience, planning, and laser-like focus.

If you can combine all three, you have a sound recipe for repeatable success.

NEW YORK, NEW YORK: FRANK SINATRA

I awoke with a start. There was the sound of a banshee ringing in my ear. I was terrified. Where was it coming from? Why was it so loud? I then realized it was loud because it was coming from me. I was screaming at the top of my voice. But why? Where was I, and why did my head throb as if I had been hit over the head with a claw hammer?

"Michael, Michael, are you okay? Can you hear me?"

"Sit up, slowly, carefully now," the voice said.

I began to get my bearings, but was in a haze. I sat up and looked round. Why was I sitting on the floor, in my suit, in an unfamiliar office, with blood dripping from my mouth?

Why were my colleagues Matt and Zack staring at me with such concerned looks?

But before I could answer these questions, I was interrupted by the sound of a broad and assertive New York accent.

"Clear away guys, let us in, the show's over, give him some air, let him breathe."

"Hi fella," the paramedic said to me, kneeling down, "how you doin'?"

And before long, still in a daze, I departed the office on a stretcher seeing a view I had never seen before, that of the 12th floor ceiling tiles.

The next twenty minutes were surreal. I was soon riding in the back of an ambulance, looking vertically up through the windows. The skyscrapers were familiar, and the noise of the streets and the accents of the paramedics reminded me of New York. But why was I in New York? And more importantly, why was I in the back of an ambulance?

"Can you tell me your name, sir?" asked the paramedic, who had hooked me up to some breathing apparatus.

I answered correctly.

"And where you live."

I answered this question correctly too.

Slowly, it was dawning on me where I was and why.

I was in New York on business.

Matt had joined me in the ambulance.

"What happened?" I asked.

"You had a fit," he said. "You scared the living daylights out of us."

He explained what had happened.

After I had tipped over, I smashed my face on the conference room floor, and began frothing at the mouth uncontrollably, and screaming at the top of my voice. I was having a seizure.

They were afraid I would swallow my tongue, and so in addition to calling the ambulance service, they attended to me to keep me out of danger. After thirty seconds or so, I calmed down, and soon after, the paramedics arrived.

I was shocked and deeply disturbed to hear this relayed back to me.

Nothing like this had ever happened before. I was fit, healthy, didn't smoke, and only drank socially. I'd felt well that morning, albeit a little jetlagged.

Anyhow, we soon arrived at the hospital. By this time I felt reasonably okay, aside from the shock of what had happened, and a throbbing mouth and headache caused by the fall and my mouth, lips and tongue taking the full impact.

For the next eight hours the staff ran tests on my heart, brain, and general condition. They concluded I had had a minor seizure but I appeared to be okay now. Based upon the tests carried out so far, there was no indication of the likely cause.

They provided me with two options: An extended stay for more comprehensive tests, or they could discharge me and leave it to me to arrange the tests on return to England. The decision was one of the easiest I have ever had to make. So, I was discharged at 3:00 a.m. and left to find a taxi back to the hotel.

I slept through to midday. When I woke, I still had a headache and a sore mouth but other than that, I felt all right.

I rang my wife Annie to tell her as delicately as possible what had happened, not, of course, wishing to alarm her. She immediately asked when I was coming home.

I hadn't even considered this. I was in New York for a purpose, and I felt that given a couple of days rest, I would be fine to travel to Pennsylvania on Wednesday evening, and lead the client meeting on Thursday that I had travelled across the Atlantic for.

She was horrified and suggested in no uncertain terms to think very carefully what I was saying.

"Your priority is not the bloody company and job, it's your health and wellbeing. I am worried sick, and I want you home."

I said she was making a fuss, and I was fine and would ring her again later.

After a wash and something to eat, I fired up the laptop, and began to work. We had a pivotal client meeting to prepare for Thursday.

I then got a call from the Sales Director in the New York office, checking on how I was, and saying I should change my flights and return home. I said thanks but no thanks: I was fine. He stressed I needed to consider my health above all else, and if I changed my mind, the office would help arrange the flight.

An hour later I got an email from the Travel Department, restating the message. Two hours after this, I received a call from the Head of HR.

She didn't hold back. She insisted I travel home immediately. In fact, it felt more like an instruction. However, as an inducement, they would book me a first class ticket.

The penny at last dropped. They wanted to offload me as soon as possible, because all the while I remained in the country, I was their responsibility.

Plus, in fairness to them, they were concerned about my welfare, and the best place for me was home in London.

I conceded, and at 9:00 a.m. the following day, I was sat in a first class seat, taking off for London Heathrow.

In addition to the luxury of first class, I had never flown through the day, always taking the "red eye" overnight, so this was a real treat.

My neighbor on the flight was no less than Damian Lewis, the star of many films and TV series, the most famous ones being *Homeland* and *Billions*.

The air stewards fussed over him, but he came across as nice, polite, unpretentious, and very patient dealing with the attention he was receiving from the flight staff.

Even though I returned to London, I still managed to participate remotely in the preparation and delivery of the presentation to the client. I'm pleased to say the sales opportunity progressed successfully to the next stage, the final outcome of which can be found in a later Section.

So why do I tell this story?

Because once again, it demonstrates resilience and tenacity, without which it is difficult to survive and prosper in sales for any length of time.

Was I loyal and committed to the company, or the role? The two inevitably get blurred. I think my main driver is a desire to succeed. I don't like to fail, especially at work.

I have a deeply ingrained work ethic, probably inherited subconsciously from my father, who travelled abroad widely throughout my childhood, and always brought work home from the office, going through papers as we watched TV together each evening.

But, and it is a big but, we also have an obligation to our loved ones.

Annie was thousands of miles away, worried out of her mind.

I did not give this the consideration it deserved.

I was wrong.

I thought the job and the impending meeting and my involvement was more important.

Worse still, I thought that without me steering the meeting in Philadelphia, we would fail.

But I was wrong.

None of us are indispensable.

I realized that soon after the client meeting finished, but did not see it at the time. I allowed my sense of loyalty to the job, and inflated opinion of myself to cloud my judgement.

I still do this, but less than I used to.

NOTE: On returning to London, I went ahead with the additional tests, but nothing showed up to explain the cause. Because of this, the consultants explained that occasionally people experience something similar to a computer rebooting, completely out of the blue, when the body shuts down, and reboots itself. Perhaps this was the explanation. The critical time would be the following two years, when I would be at my most vulnerable to a repeat.

I'm pleased to report that never happened, I feel fine, and last year decided to stop taking the preventative prescription. During that time I completed a one-day hundred-mile charity cycling event, so there have been no detectable side effects.

WHEN TWO WORLDS COLLIDE: JIM REEVES

You may be familiar with the term "sport and politics don't mix." This of course is a fallacy. Events like Colin Kaepernick's protest in 2016 and the 2022 hosting of the soccer World Cup in Qatar prove otherwise.

I mention this term because inevitably, whichever industry you work in, the world outside will intertwine with your working life.

The main ones that have affected me have been 9/11, the London bombs in 2005, the IRA terrorist threat in London during the 1990s, Israel and the Middle East, and the collapse of Lehman Brothers.

Most of us know where we were when the Twin Towers were attacked in 2001. I was in the office that day in London. While we were a predominantly UK staff, we did have one American on temporary assignment from our New York office. It was just another day, around lunch time, when out of the blue she jumped out of her seat and shouted for someone to switch on the TV immediately.

While we had a TV in the office, it was only ever turned on for special occasions, like a World Cup England football match or a royal wedding.

She had seen a news feed on her computer screen, reporting a plane had crashed into the Twin Towers in New York.

The TV was switched on and I was immediately transfixed. That said, my immediate reaction was it must have been a tragic accident. I dismissed the speculation by the commentators that it could have been planned and carried out on purpose.

And then, the second plane plowed into the side, and I immediately knew how very wrong I had been.

I was glued to the set for hours, totally drawn into the spectacle. It was an incident unprecedented in my life.

The sheer visual impact of the planes smashing into the building and the subsequent collapse have the same impact today as the first time I saw it.

The impact of the incident, however, was soon to take on a personal connection, because news began filtering through our company that our CEO and marketing manager, a single mum with a five-year-old daughter, had been due to attend an event at the Twin Towers that morning.

And so it came to pass that both perished.

The CEO, Hagay Shefi, had only recently been appointed to the role, which had required him to move his family to New York.

This personal connection gave the incident added potency for me, having only recently attended meetings with him at our headquarters in Israel.

Which leads onto London's own incident of extreme terrorism, the roots of which can be linked back to the September 11 attacks. It was Britain's leading role alongside America in bringing down Saddam Hussein in 2003 that resulted in the British being a primary target for Muslim extremists and suicide bombers.

Let me take you back to the 7th of July 2005. Britain, and especially London, is on a high following the previous day's announcement that we had been awarded the 2012 Olympics.

I am travelling into London from my home in the suburbs. The office is in the financial district of the City. I am on the district line, the green one on the tube map.

At Whitechapel station the train stops, and is held at the platform. I am still a couple of stops away from where I get off. The lights flash on and off a few times in the carriage.

After a few minutes, we are told there is an electrical fault, and we need to depart the train.

There are mumblings of frustration about the state of the trains as we head up to the exit.

Outside I decide to walk the remainder of the journey, as the queue at the bus stop is already snaking round the corner.

As I walk, I get a sense that there may be more to the "electrical fault" explanation than meets the eye. I hear sirens in the distance, more in number and louder than usual.

As I near Aldwych, the roads are blocked off and there are fire engines and ambulances surrounding the area. The police are cordoning the area off.

I continue my walk towards the office, and pass a McDonalds. It is three deep with people crowding round peering through the window to see a TV screen.

Whatever is going on, I wondered?

I soon found out.

"Reported suicide bombings on the tube. Many casualties," read the screen.

I tried calling Annie to let her know I was safe. The mobile networks were down, jammed because of the sheer volume of calls that were being made at the same time.

I continued to the office, and for the next few hours sat transfixed to the unfolding horror.

Towards the end of the morning I realized I had a client appointment scheduled for that afternoon on the other side of the City. I asked the client whether they still wanted to go ahead, and they confirmed they did.

I was shocked to say the least.

So I set off a couple of hours later on foot, and what I experienced shook me to the core.

The City was like a ghost town.

All the roads had been shut.

There was no traffic whatsoever.

There were only a handful of people out on the street.

The silence was eerie.

It wasn't until fifteen years later, and the early period of the Covid-19 pandemic and lockdown, that I experienced something similar.

A large bustling city center reduced to an eerie quiet and empty place.

I didn't personally know any of the 52 people that died that day, or the 700 plus that were injured.

I have, however, been touched by the death of colleagues three times during my career. One stands out above all else because he was my colleague during my first sales role.

Peter was his name. He was more experienced than me, a good few years older too, and we sat next to each other in the office, fulfilling a similar role to each other. Over time we got to know each other and became friends. We would often have lunch together; a bottle of red wine in a swanky City wine bar, washed down by an overpriced sandwich. Those were the days.

Over time our friendship developed such that I travelled to his home town of Liverpool, and attended a game at Anfield, the famous home of Liverpool Football Club.

Peter was single, and I think it is fair to say a maverick and unconventional sales guy. He was not everybody's "cup of tea," and very much kept himself to himself in the office.

One Monday, I arrived at work and he failed to turn up. He lived a long commute outside of London, in a quiet village near Silverstone, the home of the British Formula One Grand Prix, and had not phoned in sick.

By Wednesday my manager and I were beginning to wonder where he was. Our initial reaction of bewilderment had been replaced by one of concern.

We contacted the Personnel department for his home number (the term "HR" didn't emerge for some years after this; remember, we are in the pre-mobile phones era).

My boss called him. No answer.

The next day, still no answer.

With some trepidation, the police were notified.

By the end of the day, the news filtered through.

The police had forced their way into his house. Peter had been found dead.

They never revealed the circumstances of the death, nor the cause, and to this day, all we are left with is rumor and speculation.

His desk next to mine remained empty for months, a stark reminder each day of a loss that stayed with me for a long time and left a deep impression.

The final incident in this section was in 2008; the financial crisis and the downfall of Lehman Brothers.

I was there at Lehman Brothers' Canary Wharf offices in London that famous morning in September, and witnessed the dramatic unfolding of the story as captured by all the news channels.

I had a 10 o'clock meeting scheduled. The news had broken the previous evening, so I had no option but to turn up and contact my host from their reception area, to check whether the meeting was going ahead or not.

I knew the likelihood was low; he would have more pressing topics. But the purpose of the meeting was important, as it was the preliminary discussion on a contract for a new system.

As I sat in the reception area, large and expansive in size, I could feel the buzz of activity unfolding around me. It was fascinating to watch. I saw the team of appointed auditors arrive, about thirty in number, and get shown up to the Executive Suite on the 31st floor to start their work. They must have been notified late the previous evening when the news broke.

What I remember most, however, was a French guy who sat opposite to me on one of the sofas. He was in his late 20s, and it transpired he was due to start his new job that morning. He had uprooted himself from his home in France and a secure job to take this one. He had signed a six-month lease on a West End flat, and here was the lady from HR explaining that she was sorry, but his first day at work would not in fact be his first day at work, as the job no longer existed. He was visibly distraught. The color had drained out of his face. He was all alone in a foreign country with no job, no friends, no family, and just to rub salt into the wound the financial burden of a flat. How do I know all this? The incident was reported in one of the papers the following day.

I eventually managed to speak briefly with the guy I was meeting. He said to go and have a coffee in the café across the street and he would join me as soon as he could. Over my Americano and blueberry muffin, I watched as the staff exited the building, personal belongings in black bin liners and boxes, with the archetypal sports umbrella precariously balanced, being accosted by film crews hoping to grab a fifteen-second comment. These were the pictures transmitted all over world that evening into people's homes, and for days and weeks after.

To wrap this section up, it is to reinforce that our work does not operate in isolation of real life. A perspective is necessary, whether it is the personal friends you develop at work, or your family and friends outside. They are all human beings, vulnerable to the twists and turns of life.

DON'T LOOK UP: 2021 MOVIE STARRING LEONARDO DICAPRIO AND MERYL STREEP

Every now and then, my role in sales has resulted in meeting and mixing with some very senior people. The ones that stand out to me were the following.

The first is an American billionaire businessman, co-founder of a well-known software company. I met him in 2012 when his firm acquired the company I was working for at the time. He travelled to our headquarters in Europe, to make the announcement at a town hall style meeting and answer questions. I won't go into details but he dismissed a perfectly valid concern some of us had regarding his stated strategy and how it was going to work, when so many other firms had attempted something similar, and failed. He waved the concern away, rejecting it as irrelevant because they are who they are, and they don't ever fail.

I remember thinking the reply had come over as flippant and arrogant, but if he was the genius his background suggested, perhaps he would prove me wrong.

But he didn't. Our concerns proved correct, and the strategy had to be changed within a matter of months.

The lesson I took from this is that no matter how senior or successful someone may be, they should remain humble, listen to others, and continuously challenge their own views and opinions. No one has a monopoly on right and wrong.

Gary Hoffman is next. In 2020 he did a short stint as the Chairman of the Premier League, the most profitable soccer league in the world. Both before and after this appointment, he had held Chair and Chief Executive roles at leading financial institutions such as Monzo and Northern Rock. Northern Rock made front page news in 2007, when there was a run on the bank in the UK triggered by the credit crunch. Similar to the recent Silicon Valley Bank incident.

Our paths crossed when I was early in my sales career in the late 1980s. He was working for the firm Accenture, the business and technology consulting firm of Arthur Anderson, that was later embroiled in the 2001 Enron scandal. Despite only being in his 20s at the time, he was leading a team on a major project assignment at Barclays Bank. I was astonished how someone so young carried himself with such confidence, effortlessly speaking with senior executives at the bank, as if they were his peers. He had an X factor, and so it proved.

What I also learned from that time was the rather cynical and derogatory term I have used ever since when discussing management consulting firms, especially the large ones.

"What do consultants get paid to do?" "They borrow your watch so they can teach you the time."

While this may seem disingenuous, it was borne out on that project. The team assigned to the project were young graduates, fresh out of university, and with little or no knowledge of banking or the project's topic, a new CRM system.

It was a salient lesson, and insight into big business, which has proven valuable ever since.

Bob Greifeld served as CEO of Nasdaq between 2003 and 2016. Our paths crossed when he held a senior executive role at SunGard. In 2001, he flew to London to work with me and the team to pitch for a major project at UBS.

The final one is Sheikh Hamed bin Zayed Al Nahyan (Arabic: حامد بن زايد آل نهيان), who is an Emirati businessman and managing director of Abu Dhabi Investment Authority (ADIA). He is a member of the Al Nahyan ruling family of Abu Dhabi and the son of the late Emir (ruler) of Abu Dhabi, the founder and first president of UAE.

The ADIA contract is firmly in my top five career-best sales. The value and strategic importance of the contract was substantial.

The year was 2015. We were at the contract stage and had agreed on terms, but the commercials had yet to be negotiated.

We were caught in a dilemma.

We obviously didn't want to raise the matter with them to invite a discount discussion, but equally we were under time pressure to close the deal before year's end.

My boss and I decided we would fly to the UAE unannounced, invite ourselves to their offices, and in effect "sit there until we got the deal signed."

The tactic worked.

On Tuesday, our sponsor notified us he had arranged a meeting for us with a senior executive. The exact timing was unknown but we were told to make sure we were on hand at short notice.

Mid-afternoon that day we were notified to take the lift to one of the upper floors.

We were shown into one of the executive rooms, and left there alone.

We waited, and waited, and waited. Then there was a noise outside, and the door opened.

An entourage walked in and in the middle was, I was told, Sheikh Hamed.

We didn't know it was him, but were left in no doubt that he was a very important person and without his approval, the deal would not go ahead.

We recognized only one of the entourage, our senior sponsor.

We had not been told explicitly what was expected of the meeting.

Was this going to be a meet and greet, or something more substantial? We had no idea.

There was no small talk. The Sheikh asked a handful of very pertinent questions about the project.

He then asked us how we could improve the offer. Just like that.

No justification, no explanation.

I will admit that I felt intimidated and nervous.

It was the way the meeting had been set up, all shrouded in mystery. Then the nature of the grand entrance, combined with the gravitas of the executive. Add to the mix the unfamiliar surroundings of an unfamiliar culture, the robes, and the office protocols. Everything combined to create this feeling of uncertainty, mystery, and the unknown.

I promptly proposed a reasonable level of discount, with a short justification.

He seemed satisfied with this and in less than five minutes the meeting was over.

I left the meeting a nervous wreck. My underarms were soaking wet under my suit jacket.

It had been unnerving, and I was drained of all mental energy.

Thankfully, years of experience had enabled me to hold it all together, just, and the contract was signed a few days later.

SLIDING DOORS: 1998 MOVIE STARRING GWYNETH PALTROW / 12 ANGRY MEN: 1957 MOVIE STARRING HENRY FONDA

The *Sliding Doors* movie of 1998 starring Gwyneth Paltrow is the backdrop of this story. I am convinced that if it hadn't been for a particular set of events, the outcome of a bid I was involved in in 2016 would have turned out very differently and would have had wider consequences for me, the group I worked in at the time, and a handful of individuals.

I have already spoken about the incident I experienced in New York. Well, the client I was scheduled to pitch to that week in Philadelphia is the same client at the heart of this story.

As you recall, we made it through to the next round, which was to be the RFP stage, an invitation to five potential suppliers to issue full commercial proposals.

That said, it is worth quickly sharing with you what went before this. I was new in the role. I joined the company in the January of that year. What I discovered, however, had shocked me. The state of the business I had been hired to shake up and set on a new direction was far worse than I had expected. This is covered in more detail elsewhere.

Suffice it to say we discovered a potential opportunity with one of the company's US major financial services accounts. As part of their due diligence, they issued us a short questionnaire.

I shared the questions with the product support team. They read them and immediately started panicking. "We can't do this, we can't do that, we don't have the type of client references they're asking for, the product isn't even finished yet," and so on.

But I was not going to be deterred. My task was to win new business sales. The pipeline of opportunities I had inherited was threadbare at best so there was no way I was going to turn this opportunity down without a fight.

So, I had to spend hours working through the questions, reminding the team that there are different ways the questions could be interpreted, so we could respond more positively than they were originally thinking.

This is standard business practice. Clients always set out their stall of requirements to be the "Rolls Royce" version. What I didn't expect was my colleagues to panic the minute something difficult presented itself. I was going to have to manage this team much more closely than I had expected. They appeared both naïve and inexperienced, which was worrying and draining on my time.

I was also picking up mumblings of discontent reflecting the sentiment that "Michael's another typical salesman, breezes in from outside, thinks he knows best, willing to sell and say anything to make a quick buck, whether it works or not. Completely untrustworthy."

I knew that unless I addressed this promptly, this distrust would build and escalate like wildfire, which wouldn't have been good for anyone.

This image of salespeople has of course been around since the dawn of time. In some industries and with some individuals it is legitimate, but in most cases it is quite frankly ridiculous. And this includes me. Once people have worked with me for a while, they realize I can be trusted. I do not ask or expect anyone to be untruthful, but there is a game to be played. There are different ways of answering questions without saying no or appearing unable to meet requirements. And while I will support and defend colleagues in the face of client requests and demands, they also need to step up to the mark. It needs to cut both ways.

So, an element of toughness and determination was required for this group. There was a need for them to change, which they would no doubt resist unless I handled it firmly. It needed vision and leadership.

Anyhow, we put together a response to the questions, massaged some of the answers as required, and awaited a reply from the client. It came back within a few days, and the answer was positive. We would be invited to respond to the formal RFP. I was delighted.

The RFP arrived a week or so later, with a scope that was both broad and comprehensive. There were lots of detailed questions, and many sections covering a range of topics. I had managed many of these over the years, and it is like any elephant task. You put together a core team, break the response down into manageable sets, allocate different sections to different people, put together a plan of deadlines, and manage the process closely.

But my goodness, this was like dealing with kindergarten children. They were so out of their depth it was disturbing. The realization hit me quickly. I would need to oversee all the sections at a level of detail I had not expected. Full delegation was not going to work.

The deadline for submission was the Friday following the August Monday bank holiday. I mention this because I had been assigned jury duty during the last two weeks of August, which meant I wouldn't be in the office to oversee matters.

While this was less than ideal, I was not unduly fazed. I thought it would be manageable, as I could work from home in the evenings after jury service, and my colleague Matt, who I could rely upon, was in the office with the team. Plus, I had no option. I couldn't get out of jury service, so I would have to make it work.

But it was a concern. The RFP was complex, we only had a short time window in which to respond, and as we have discussed, the team was not the quality and experience I would have liked.

It is at moments like this in life that fate sometimes plays a part. The *Sliding Doors* moment. And this was very much the case here. Let me explain.

It was two weeks before we needed to submit the proposal. On Monday I turned up for jury duty and sat around for two and half days without being called. Then Wednesday at lunch time I was assigned a case, not a serious one. A guy was accused of fraud for using a neighbor's Disabled Badge to park his car near his place of work.

By Friday morning the evidence and arguments finished, and we were asked to retire to consider our verdict.

Allow me to digress, for a moment.

I am sure you have often been asked "what is your favorite film?" It's a great topic of conversation with friends.

I have three. They are *Kes*, an iconic British working-class film from the late 60s, *The Usual Suspects* with Kevin Spacey, and *12 Angry Men*, which is a 50s American film with a youthful-looking Henry Fonda in the lead.

The essence of *12 Angry Men*, if you are not familiar with it, is that Fonda plays the wise, considered, quiet, but deeply determined juror who wants to ensure justice is done. The accused is an 18-year-old immigrant kid, charged with killing his father. The film is based in New York. The evidence looks overwhelming against the boy. The jurors, all of them men, convene in the jury room and elect a chairman.

As often in cases such as these, the 12 are the classic mix and blend of characters, which include some that are outspoken and convinced of the verdict without the need for any further debate. Namely, that the boy is undoubtedly guilty. "What's the point of debating it, let's have a show of hands, agree unanimously that he is guilty, and get home." From memory, the Yankees were playing that evening, and one of the jurors had tickets. You get the picture.

Henry is the lone voice. He says they should at least debate the verdict, and surely the boy deserves this as a minimum. He reasonably suggests that why not give everyone an opportunity to speak and express their thoughts and observations, and whether they were concerned with any aspects of the case and evidence.

If after this, everyone agrees the defendant is guilty, then fine.

He is shouted down, but eventually a few others agree, and so the film follows the way in which the room moves from a unanimous vote of guilty to a unanimous vote of not guilty. It's wonderful, and if you have never seen it, I strongly recommend it.

This film immediately came to mind as we sat down to discuss and consider our case.

There are a number of traits and personality types that I do not warm to. Among these are bullies, bigots, and loudmouths. I have been brought up with the strong belief of giving people a voice, and that no one person's opinion is more important or valuable than another.

So, when this loudmouth, self-opinionated, London black-cab driver starts off on his rant that "the guy is guilty, it's obvious, this is the most open and shut case he has ever seen," I thought of the film, and the need for a firm hold on this jury process. I was not prepared to stand by and see him dominate proceedings. I wanted a considered debate, where everyone felt able to express their views and feelings. Furthermore, the accused was not English, which made me even more determined to ensure this loudmouth was not going to steamroller his way through proceedings.

As well as wishing to see matters were handled "fairly," I had two other main fears.

One, was that the odious taxi driver would volunteer to be the Chairman, and two, that if he were Chairman, he would alienate and bully some of the others. This, in a weird way, could drag out the debate because his manner could provoke argument and opposition for the sake of it. I had neither the time nor the patience for this.

Plus, it was a boiling hot day outside, it was the Friday before the bank holiday, and I wanted to get home. I didn't want to be stuck in a dingy jury room any longer than necessary.

So, when it was put to the room who would like to be Chairman, and he was the only one that put himself forward, without hesitation, I volunteered myself. I won by a landslide, much to my relief, and I suspect to most of the others in the room.

So, I led the process, asked everyone to express their initial thoughts, and set out a plan of how we should consider the evidence and arrive at a conclusion.

I could sense there was a mix in the room, some in no hurry for the case to be handled efficiently and concluded, and those that wanted the complete opposite and didn't care that much whether they fulfilled their responsibilities honorably or not.

Navigating between the two was going to need all my years of experience, and firm diplomacy.

We have all seen enough police, court-based TV shows to know a mountain of evidence is presented during a case, much of it red herrings and not materially relevant. The key, I have always felt, is to focus on the handful of big issues, which materially influence the probability of whether the accused is guilty or not guilty.

So, we spent two productive hours debating the subject. The initial feeling at the outset, when I suggested we do a straw poll, was nine to three in favor of a guilty verdict. For the record I was convinced that he was guilty, but the prosecuting lawyer had performed so poorly that he allowed the defendant to present a case that appeared far more nuanced and less compelling than I felt it was.

The debate amongst the jurors proved extremely valuable, the few stragglers that were concerned with certain aspects of the case were slowly convinced, and we settled on a unanimous guilty verdict.

It is interesting that the term we hear consistently in these shows is "beyond reasonable doubt." It is an immensely powerful phrase. You get presented with this mountain of evidence and anecdotes, a lot of which doesn't make sense. Either someone is lying, or someone has forgotten something, or claims to have seen something but in fact didn't because their mind has played a trick on them, and so on.

It's this term "beyond reasonable doubt" that enables cases to be concluded, because without it, there would never be a conclusion to a case.

So, it was this concept that saved the debate dragging on longer than was necessary.

By three o'clock, we had agreed unanimously that the defendant was guilty and notified the court of our verdict. The judge thanked us and asked us to return to the central waiting room, to await our next case.

As we began to return to the waiting area, we were halted in our tracks, and an official of the court came and addressed us. "Because of the time of year," she said, "the number of cases scheduled for next week is less than usual, and therefore you are surplus to requirements. You are therefore being released a week early, and do not need to attend next week. Have a good weekend."

I was delighted.

As a short aside, also attending the court that week as a juror was the film actor Ben Whishaw. He is a favorite of mine and I love all the work he has done. That said, I am a hopeless "spotter" of famous people, but I saw him hanging around the waiting room on Monday, and thought it looked like him.

You may know him for being Q in the James Bond films, such as *Skyfall*. For the British audience, he also appeared in *A Very English Scandal* with Hugh Grant, about the disgraced politician Jeremy Thorpe.

On the Tuesday after the Bank Holiday, I travelled down to the Tunbridge Wells office where the team was located, arriving about 8:30 a.m.

By 10 o'clock I thanked fate for the hand it had dealt me. Why do I say this? Because if I had not been there on-site to manage those final days of producing the Proposal, we would either have missed the deadline and been disqualified from the bid, or the quality would have been so poor it would have lessened the chances of progressing any further.

That week, I worked all the hours available, getting up before six every morning, travelling two hours down to the office, working through the day on all aspects of the bid, leaving the office at six, proofreading on the train into Cannon Street, arriving home at eight, having supper with Annie, and then working a couple more hours before retiring to bed. It was exhausting, especially cajoling the team to provide the necessary information to a quality I could work with.

Despite all this, I was really pleased with the Proposal we finally submitted. And most importantly, it went in on time, albeit with only one hour to go before the deadline. Talk about "Just in time operations."

While the client reviewed the responses, I considered our chances. On the one hand, the reply we had submitted was of decent quality, and our relationship with the client was good, because we supplied systems to them in other parts of their organization. But on the downside, the system we were proposing was new and still under development, and we had not been on the original list to receive the RFP, because the client thought our technology out of date and not comparable with other suppliers.

However, after two weeks, a decision was announced. Much to our surprise, and excitement, we had been shortlisted with one other supplier.

I was surprised primarily because the system was so new, and the operation they wanted it for was a strategic part of their business.

We were invited to workshop an on-site Proof of Concept over three days in December in Philadelphia. We had six weeks to prepare, rehearse, and complete. I knew immediately we would need every minute.

The preparation was particularly challenging for a range of reasons.

Three days is a long time to spend with one client, on one product and service. The level of detail we would need to cover was going to be substantial.

This was made more difficult because the software was still under development and incomplete in a number of areas that we needed to show during the workshop.

And finally, we hadn't yet sold and implemented the system for any other clients, so a lot of the knowledge and information we were going to present was both untested and "in theory," without any proof to back it up.

Anyhow, that December we travelled to Philadelphia and delivered one of the most outstanding, albeit stressful, three-day workshops I have had the honor to lead. I acted as compere, or master of ceremonies. I was continually alert for signs that the guys were struggling and under pressure so I could step in and deflect attention away from them, while they resolved whatever problems they had and regained their composure.

Somehow, we managed to get through it relatively unscathed, and by the end, the client seemed happy.

The sales process continued through February, when we were eventually notified that we were the preferred supplier of the two, and would be invited to exclusively negotiate contract terms and conditions.

While this took a further four months to complete, the client eventually signed a $3.75 million contract.

That said, it involved some anxious moments along the way. One in particular sticks in my mind.

I was in New Jersey, hosting a two-day workshop with a different client. It was June. The aforementioned contracts and commercial proposals had been agreed, and we were now waiting for it to work its way through the decision-making and approval process in the higher echelons of the organization. A contract of this size and strategic importance would typically need the approval of a Board Director.

During an afternoon break, I checked my phone for emails and messages, and spotted a news announcement I couldn't believe. The CEO had announced his resignation. A wave of negative thoughts began drifting through my mind. One was that all projects and investments would be put on hold until a new CEO was in place, and had reviewed and agreed all current initiatives.

Such concerns were not unreasonable. I had been on the receiving end of them in the past, some of which had turned out disastrously, with contracts at an advanced stage being abandoned. I immediately rang the account manager to see if he knew anything more than was in the press. He didn't, he was as surprised as me, and said he would check it out.

We soon discovered the new CEO was an internal appointment, and the transition would be over a six-month period. I managed to relax a little and feel more confident. The new leader would in all likelihood be aware and supportive of the various investments budgeted for that year. So the worst case would be a delay, with senior executives and directors distracted for a while.

And so it proved. After an anxious two weeks, the contract was approved, and an Agreement signed.

The deal attracted plaudits from the company's senior management. For me, it was proof that the strategy and approach I had set out in 2016 when I joined could deliver results.

It was one of the proudest sales of my career. The champagne celebration that night with Annie was one I remember to this day.

So what do we take from this? Two things. Fate can play an important part in our successes and failures. And when it is time to step up and lead, do not shun that responsibility. Grab it, and own it.

TALES OF THE UNEXPECTED: ROALD DAHL

It pays to expect the unexpected. Two experiences come to mind.

The first was in 2004. At the time, I was the country manager for a software company, with an office in London. My third hire was a sales guy. We'll call him Paul. A salesperson of some experience, he had learned his trade in large corporations and was in his 50s, more than ten years my senior.

We were an early-stage firm, so neither of us were expected to be winning too many deals initially. But a year in, two things struck me and frustrated me about his performance.

The first was he seemed old fashioned in his approach. He'd failed to adapt to the needs of the current marketplace and the different ways of selling.

The second and more important frustration was he was not closing any business. His pipeline of opportunities seemed stuck, with few of them progressing through the funnel.

We did weekly reviews, but I had purposely hired him for his experience so I wouldn't need to get too involved in his work, because I had my own sales target to hit.

So I discussed the situation with the CEO and he agreed with my recommendation; we should let him go.

Decisions like this are not easy. I can remember a number of things going through my mind at the time.

The sentiment that he's a really nice guy, and he is trying his best.

But this was soon replaced by a steely determination that he is a sales guy, he needs to sell, and if he doesn't then he must expect the consequences.

That said, if I sacked him, I would need to hire a replacement, which would be tiresome, and time consuming.

And finally, there was the niggling thought: "would he manage to get another job?" If others viewed him the way I did, and you combined this with his age, then he could find it really difficult to find another role.

However, putting this all to one side, I put in place the necessary paperwork, and arranged for us to meet one Tuesday, first thing. He had taken the Friday and Monday off.

When he walked into the office that Tuesday, he pulled me to one side and said he needed to talk to me about something.

I was momentarily thrown off my stride.

At the back of my mind, I was hoping that maybe he was about to resign!

He then announced he had not been feeling well recently and the reason for his long weekend was to enable him to undergo tests in a hospital. The outcome was not great. He had dangerously high blood pressure and the doctor had prescribed him some drugs and instructions not to overdo it, but most important of all, avoid stressful situations.

My heart sank. While I was sorry Paul's health was not great, I was now facing a dilemma. Do I go through with the meeting and explain he was being let go?

Wouldn't I feel callous and insensitive if I did?

What if dismissing him triggered a heart attack and he collapsed in front of me?

I had a split second to decide.

And then he spoke. "What did you want to talk to me about, Michael?"

I said it was nothing that couldn't wait and switched the conversation back to him.

The doctor had instructed him to take a couple of weeks off, which he did.

On his return, we reconvened the meeting.

I couldn't delay it any further.

I knew I had to go ahead with the dismissal, and within a couple of weeks he was out.

As it turned out, I was lucky.

The exit was amicable.

He was a proud sales guy and knew his performance was not acceptable, so he understood why the company had to do what it did.

Furthermore, he had been so embarrassed about his performance that he hadn't claimed any expenses for over a year. He had calculated the amount owed, and it ran into the thousands!

When he told me I was speechless. How could someone do this?

So we agreed on a compromise. We would proceed as agreed with his dismissal and a couple of months' money, and he would waive his right to claim the expenses retrospectively.

He left the following week, his health improved, and I noticed on LinkedIn he managed to get himself another job within a few months. So all ended well.

The second anecdote is more recent, from 2016. In January of that year, I started with a large US software company. I had been headhunted by them, to come in and reenergize an underperforming business unit.

I had done a reasonable amount of due diligence before accepting the role, but I soon discovered I had badly underestimated the task. This is covered in the section Sliding Doors.

I spent day one at headquarters and then arranged to travel to the office where the business unit was based for the remainder of the week. I was keen to appraise the state of the business, see the product in action, meet the team, learn about the clients, and assess the quality of the sales pipeline.

By close of business on Wednesday, I felt deeply disturbed.

I had spent a great deal of that time with the Managing Director (MD), and my impression was not at all good.

He was an old school, traditional, ex-army type, an outwardly looking smart, astute businessperson. But he seemed clueless. I could not discover a single redeeming feature or meaningful contribution he was making. He had allowed the business unit to crash and burn.

But who to confide in? Was I the only one to feel like this? Surely not.

My direct boss was back at HQ, and I wasn't due back there until the following Monday.

The guy I did know, but not that well, was Matt, who had first approached me about the job. But he was difficult to read.

I had met with him on Tuesday a couple of times on different topics, and he had shown no signs of concern or frustration with the MD or the situation the business was in.

But I had no option. I would need to speak with Matt and deal with the fallout if there was one.

I asked if he would like to meet the following day for breakfast.

He accepted and the next day, over coffee and toast I broached the subject.

I felt really nervous, and remember how difficult I had found it to concentrate on the train that morning.

Much to my relief he immediately agreed with my observations. And then followed a barrage of criticisms and frustrations that he had bottled up for months.

I continued the rest of the week with meetings with the various staff, and by the Friday I had a reasonable preliminary grasp of the business, what needed to change, and the outline of a sales strategy.

During the afternoon, I received a call from my boss at headquarters. He said he wanted me to present to him and the Vice President of Sales on the Tuesday at 9 a.m.

They wanted to hear my sales strategy and plan for the business. I queried why so soon, as I had only been there a matter of days, but he insisted. The MD would be invited too.

So, I put the materials together on the Monday, and was in the London office by 8:00 on Tuesday. By 8:30 the MD had not turned up, and my boss casually mentioned that he had been delayed and might in fact not get there at all.

Now don't ask me what made me think this smelled fishy, but I clearly remember thinking that of all the meetings the MD would want and need to attend, it was this one. For a host of reasons. It just seemed strange.

At 9:00, my boss and the VP of Sales strode in and announced the MD had been relieved of his duties and was no longer with the company.

I don't mind admitting I was taken off guard. But I quickly regained my composure and presented my plan.

By the end they fully approved of my approach, thanked me, told me to just get on with it, and if I needed anything, to let them know. Just like that. As if nothing out of the ordinary had happened.

Reflecting back on this incident, I remember leaving the meeting feeling ten feet tall.

But why?

By this stage of my career, I was a proven salesperson. After all, they wouldn't have hired me otherwise.

So why did I feel so proud?

It took a while to work out, but I think there was an element of imposter syndrome. The US firm at the time had a terrific reputation, that they only hired the very best salespeople in the business.

Furthermore, I hadn't worked for a large corporation for over twenty years. This felt like proof that I could add the same amount of value to a company this size, with its wealth of staff and resources, as I had done to the smaller, early-stage companies I had worked for over the previous twenty years.

It felt good.

THE TEARS OF A CLOWN: SMOKEY ROBINSON & THE MIRACLES

At a certain time in our lives, most of us are forced to face a set of circumstances and events that really test our inner resilience, and in doing so, help to form us into the people we become.

Annie and I losing our only son William at the age of thirteen is mine.

He died on his bike one dark morning in November, hit by a car while doing his paper round before school.

I will never forget the moment there was a knock on the front door, and there at 7:30 in the morning stood a lone policeman with a grave look on his face.

The air disappeared out of my body in an instant. We rushed out of the house to the hospital. The image of William's breakfast standing on the side cabinet—Marmite on toast, a cup of tea, and a bowl of cereal—will stay with me forever.

This tale will focus on the business perspective, rather than the impact on my personal life.

So, one of the earliest decisions I needed to make was whether or not to cancel a job interview that was scheduled for the following week.

At the time, I was out of work.

I was inclined to go ahead with the interview, and Annie agreed; we both needed things to distract us from the enormity of what we were facing. Preparing for the interview would be one such distraction.

So the following week, I travelled to Dublin, met the owners of the company, and subsequently received an offer. The start date would be the first day in January.

That first week was the most emotionally draining week of my life, bar none.

It was freezing cold in Dublin, and on Monday, I duly arrived at the company's office in a dark, dank industrial estate.

The people were welcoming and excited I had joined. The firm was an early-stage software company that had hired me to head up sales and set up an office in London to target the UK financial services market.

For the entirety of the trip there, and all through Christmas, I was trying to decide how I would answer the question: "Do you have children?" An innocent enough question.

On the one hand, I could answer truthfully, and explain that my son had recently died, so I no longer had children. But this didn't feel right. I was going to be meeting people for the first time, and this was no way to begin building relationships.

I could just answer no, and leave it at that.

Or I could answer yes, but not elaborate that he was no longer alive. This of course was absurd.

I was leaning towards option 2. I could deal with the details of William's loss as I got to know people better.

So this is what I did.

I managed to get through the first day relatively unscathed, throwing myself into my work, learning lots of new things and meeting different people.

In the evening I set off for the guest house that had been booked for me. It was a fifteen-minute walk. There was ice and snow on the ground from a snowfall the previous week.

I found the place on a dark, badly lit residential road. I rang the bell, but nobody answered.

I telephoned the number, but got no reply. I could hear it ringing on the other side of the door.

Frustrated and irritated, I went off to a bar to escape the cold, and returned thirty minutes later. Still no answer. There were lights on but no movement inside.

I then realized I hadn't got the telephone number of the Finance Officer who had made the booking.

I felt unsure what to do.

The company was a start-up that had already made it clear costs and expenses were tightly managed. I knew I was not in the best state of mind and didn't want to go to another place, incur extra costs, and get off on the wrong foot.

But I was cold, hungry, with a heavy suitcase. And all I wanted was to get warm and curl up into a ball and cry.

Suddenly, I heard a voice from behind me. It was the owner.

She muttered an apology, explained she had had to go somewhere in a hurry, and opened up. The place was a dump. Old, in need of decoration, and devoid of atmosphere.

Within a few minutes I was safely in my bedroom, which matched the rest of the guest house: Cramped, with a rock-hard bed, and radiator heat that was patchy at best. The towels were hard, crusty, and threadbare.

I spent the evening crying uncontrollably, unable to concentrate on reading or watching TV. I went through a whole box of tissues. My feelings of grief were intense.

How I got through that week I will never know.

Each morning it felt like I had to put on an imaginary mask and wear it throughout the day.

Nobody knew the burden I was carrying, and thank goodness for that, because it would have made my job untenable at that time.

I look back on that week and wonder how I managed to survive. The circumstances could not have been more challenging. A new job, meeting with people I didn't know, the need to learn new information, being away from home, holed up in a dank, unwelcoming guest house, and carrying the burden of the loss of my son with no one to speak to.

The most troubling aspect was carrying that huge secret. I was unable to relax or feel at ease in the office, for fear of breaking down or saying the wrong thing. I remember excusing myself a few times to visit the toilet, to "collect myself."

I had to erect a barrier between myself and everyone I met, for fear they would ask personal questions.

By the end of each day, I was emotionally exhausted.

Somehow, I pulled through and slowly became stronger. But it took me years to settle on and feel at ease with an answer to the aforementioned question.

Before then I experimented with many different versions.

When I answered a straight no, I don't have children, I felt it was a betrayal of William. He deserved better. He had a life. He did exist. He still did in my heart, and to dismiss this with a curt "no," didn't feel at all right.

So eventually, I became confident enough in myself to answer the question with, "No, my son died a few years ago." I knew the risks. It could kill the mood of a conversation, which in sales was less than ideal.

It could also make the other person very uncomfortable and feel they had pried into my personal life. But so what? Honoring William's memory was more important than either, and if that meant my career in sales was unsustainable, then so be it.

Which is where we are today. I still get a mix of reactions. The main one is a quick acknowledgement, a muttered apology, and a change of subject, which is fine. Some bold ones ask about the circumstances, such as how long ago it was or how old he was, but not much more than that.

The lesson I drew from this experience is this. Until it happens to us, we have no idea how we will react or manage when faced by extreme adversity. While I managed to get through the loss of William, I cannot imagine dealing with a vast range of other things. Like being a citizen of Ukraine and being bombed and having my home and country destroyed, or seeing up close the aftermath of a major road incident. For others, the thought of losing a child is beyond their comprehension.

Since the loss, I have seen the world through a very different lens. Stressful periods at work and in my home life are easier to manage, and I feel I am a more compassionate and empathetic person than I was before.

While I haven't lost my determination and tenacity to succeed, I do believe I am a more rounded personality, which has benefited me both at work and in my personal life.

By way of example, I have volunteered for a couple of charities since William died. The first was with teenagers that had lost a parent, while for the last five years or more, I have been providing helpline support for bereaved parents.

CHUTZPAH

"Hi, boss."

"How did it go, Michael?" he asked.

"I've got good news, and bad news. Which would you like first?"

"I don't care, just tell me," he said a little impatiently.

"Well," I continued, "the good news is I got them to confirm we have been selected as the preferred supplier, and they want to go ahead."

"Excellent. And the bad news?"

"They want to visit the offices in Dublin, and check out that we are a bona fide company, and not just a couple of fellas working out of a shed in an industrial estate."

There was silence on the line.

"No problem, Michael, just leave it to me, you just focus on getting the deal through."

And that was it. Very matter of fact, no pondering aloud how we were going to manage this. Nothing, just plain and simple, "Leave it to me, I will sort it."

And that pretty much summed up Martin, the CEO. Pragmatic, and a doer.

So why mention this? What's the big deal about a client visit?

The year is 2009. We are a niche Irish software company. I am the country manager in the UK, leading sales in the UK, our primary market.

Our main targets were the larger banks.

So, while we were a "bona fide" company, I had always given the impression to prospects that we were larger than we were. At the time we had less than twenty staff; I felt we needed to be twice this size.

Also, the office quite frankly was a bit rundown. It was drab and uninspiring and reminded me of a sixties "public office," rather than a dynamic financial software company.

The biggest issue, however, was the number of staff. How were we going to overcome this hurdle? Our visitors were a major UK bank. But I had implicit faith in Martin and had pretty much put the issue out of my mind. If he said, "leave it to me," then that's what I did.

So, on the day of the visit, I took the first flight out of London to Dublin and arrived in the office at just after 9:00 a.m. We'd agreed on the topics with the client, booked a nice lunch venue, and arranged proper coffee and posh biscuits; we were all set. They were due to arrive at 11:00.

The office was on the second floor of a four-story building. As you came in the front door, you had to turn either right or left, and small rooms led off from the narrow corridors. It was not a modern, open design.

To the left were the technical and support teams, and to the right sales, marketing, and admin. On entering the office there was a reception desk straight in front of you, but it was always empty, as we had no need for a reception-ist. But that day was different

On this morning, a delightful young woman greeted me from a spruced-up reception desk. "Hello, how can I help you?"

I have to admit being taken completely by surprise, and mumbling out something like, "Oh, I work here, I'm from the London office; is Martin in?"

She brightly answered, "Of course," and showed me to his office.

Once the receptionist had returned to her desk, I blurted out, "What the hell is going on? Who is she?"

"Hired for the day," he said, beaming like the cat that got the cream. "Like it?"

"Impressive" I said. "What else have you done?"

"Come this way I'll show you." We walked down the opposite corridor to the meeting room. "Welcome to the boardroom," he said. And lo and behold, there was this stunning table, sitting center stage. It looked fantastic and was clearly not a cheap purchase. We obviously meant business.

As we walked down the corridor, I noticed a worrying number of empty seats where the regular staff sat. I soon discovered the gods were against us. It was "Sod's Law," or maybe I should say, "Murphy's Law." On this day of all days, some staff were sick, others on holiday, and others onsite with a client. The rooms were as deserted as the deck of the Marie Celeste.

"That doesn't look good, Martin," I said. "The empty seats are in full view of the corridor we need to walk down with the bank to the boardroom."

"You worry too much, Michael, come and see."

He led me down the opposite corridor that was my main area of concern. I was deeply worried the clients would want to walk around and meet some of the staff. The opposite end of the office we were heading down had two problems. One: it was an area piled up with broken, unused old screens and PCs, and other technology junk. The other: nobody worked in that area because it was spare office space, for when we grew and hired more people.

Well, was I in for a surprise! The minute I had finished my aforementioned call with Martin announcing the need to arrange the visit, he had sent out an internal note to all the Dublin staff.

"Urgent Request. Crate of Beer Reward"
To all Dublin-based staff

We need to fill out the office with people for a client visit. Contact your friends, family, neighbors. Anyone available to spend a morning at our offices, working at a computer screen, will be reimbursed with their travel expenses, and a crate of beer. Please apply.

And that was it. The response had been overwhelming and here we were, a tidy office, screens cleaned and stood up right, turned on, and a miscellaneous range of friends and family, pretending to be building the next version of product!

The visit went off like a dream, the clients went home happy, and the deal was signed a few weeks later.

Irish blarney at its finest. Or as they say in Yiddish, "chutzpah."

CULTURE CLUB (PIONEERING 1980S POP BAND FRONTED BY BOY GEORGE)

The topic of culture is an important one, aligned as it is with current trends towards improved wellbeing.

Being an industry veteran who entered sales in the late 1980s, I am a keen advocate. I've experienced both good and bad, and back when I started, the topic was never spoken about.

In the sales office I worked in as a rookie, I was the victim of bullying a number of times, but it never crossed my mind to raise it with my management or complain. It was just part and parcel of the workplace. It was implicitly implied that if you were not a strong enough character to handle it, then you probably weren't suited for the "cut and thrust" of sales.

As I previously mentioned, prior to launching my sales consultancy practice, I worked for a large US corporation, employing in excess of 50,000 staff. To their credit, the People's Office issued an annual staff questionnaire that provided the opportunity for all staff to anonymously comment and grade the company on a range of topics, some of which related to the broad term, "culture."

However, the day-to-day reality rarely reconciled with the positive results.

The one incident that has remained with me occurred in 2017 at the company's annual sales kickoff in Florida. It had no bearing upon general wellbeing and involved no bullying or discriminatory behavior, but for me it very much reflected a certain culture.

The kickoff was attended by the global salesforce drawn from all regions of the world except the Middle East and Africa,

The venue was bizarre. It was a Disney-themed hotel!

A ten-minute walk from the Epcot Center, it was right in the middle of the main tourist area. The hotel shop was full of Disney memorabilia, and there were families walking around in T-shirts and flip flops, with the kids wearing Mickey Mouse costumes at breakfast.

At one of the general sessions, the members of the Board were given an opportunity to sit on stage and have a conversation about their insight into the industry. One of the Directors was asked to open up to the audience and say something about herself before covering some business topics.

That this Director in question was a woman was a positive factor, because there are not many female executives in major technology companies. And she was unconventional. In her mid-50s and elegant, she dressed in bold, stylish clothes, and had bright peroxide spikey hair.

Her character very much fitted her "punky" appearance. She was loud, and very outspoken.

All in all, I felt she was an incredibly positive asset to the company. That said, her outbursts were quite famous too, so for a publicly listed corporation to support and promote such a character, I thought was good.

The CEO of this multi-billion dollar company was excellent too. He had been with the company for over thirty years, started as a junior computer programmer, and worked himself up through the organization. He always delivered the keynote speech to open the conference, and he was terrific. Humble, articulate, amusing, and super smart, he seemed like an approachable, down-to-earth family man.

Returning to the aforementioned Director, the interviewer asked the executive: "So, tell the good people out here a little bit about yourself, outside of work, what are your hobbies?" She threw her head back, and nonchalantly answered, "I haven't really thought about it, Chuck. I like doing normal things, you know, going out to dinner, meeting up with friends, that sort of thing."

The interviewer persisted, saying she must have hobbies or passions; what were they?

And to this day, I don't know whether this was scripted or not, because they must surely have prepared the questions beforehand. Anyhow, she answered, "I like buying houses. I am just in the process of buying my fifth!"

Dear reader, I kid you not. This is no lie.

This triggered two very distinct responses from the audience of two thousand or so delegates.

The first, from the American contingent, was a whoop and cheer. The implication was "Yeah, that is great, she is a high achiever and has been so successful she can afford to buy lots of houses. This is a cause for celebration. This is what we aspire to achieve. This is living the American dream."

The other reaction, which I have to say was the more overwhelming one, was a stunned silence and take-in of breath, along the lines of "Wow! Did I really hear that correctly?" "Her hobby is buying houses? What sort of hobby is that?"

This is not to say I am criticizing US salespeople. I am not. But even if I were a good US sales guy, earning say $200,000 a year plus commission, I would still be thinking, "I have three kids going through school and college. I have taxes to pay, a mortgage, I'm frequently in conflict with the company over expenses and sales targets, and this woman is sitting here on stage, earning goodness knows how many millions a year, and her hobby is buying houses! I can just about afford a week away by the coast and a few long weekends down at my parents-in-law."

"Why doesn't she have regular hobbies like painting, or playing golf?"

On speaking with some of the UK guys afterwards, a number of which were under 35, the sentiment was very much: "Has she any idea how crass and disconnected from real life that sounded? I can't afford to get on the housing ladder, because the cost of property is so high. My only opportunity will be if I inherit my parents' money, and that is years away, because they are so fit and healthy."

Now, I am neither American nor under 35, and I am financially secure, but I felt sick to my stomach. How could someone this smart say something so fundamentally boorish? It was breathtaking. But what it did was demonstrate the risks companies run when they build up multiple layers of management, and the senior executives lose touch with the staff.

This symptom is of course currently prevalent across many companies and societies, and is undermining trust, unity, and community.

The culture of a company can usually be traced back to the top executive. But as the company gets bigger, it is often dictated by the head of a business division.

The one I worked for, I felt, was toxic. The European VP of Sales only surrounded himself with yes men and women. He was rarely seen on the "sales floor," remaining aloof and distant except for occasional town hall meetings.

A great many good salespeople joined and left within a couple of years, frustrated at the lack of meritocracy and worse.

A telling indictment was the graduate scheme the company invested in, training more than twenty of the brightest talents in the industry, only to see the vast majority leave within three years of joining. Such a waste, and just one example of the impact a poor culture can have on an organization.

I personally experienced bullying during the last couple of years at the company. I didn't do much about it. I didn't want to report it, because this would have alienated me even further, and deep down I probably didn't feel it would have had much effect.

The executive that I felt was bullying me was a woman based in Boston, who seemed to revel in the power her seniority bestowed upon her. She expressed little or no emotion and showed no appreciation to members of staff that worked with her. The question is whether she was exploiting this "power" and authority to intimidate and bully, or was it just her management style? In my view, I think it was exploitation and bullying. Others may disagree.

As an amusing aside, or should I say a black humor moment, one September she was visiting from the States for a week. She had a range of meetings arranged, one of which was with me in Dublin, to meet a disgruntled client.

The meeting was at 2:00 p.m. Her meeting prior to this, without me, was with a client for whom we were bidding a major transformation project. I was the lead salesperson on the bid. The meeting didn't go well and we were criticized for a particular stance we were taking.

So when she and I convened prior to the afternoon meeting to prepare, she was in a foul mood. She blamed me for the morning meeting going badly, which was uncalled for, and told me she had no intention of conceding any of the complaints the afternoon client had, even though I had explained how reasonable some of them were.

And so it proved. The meeting was most unsatisfactory, I was forced to follow her line of argument, and the client left feeling more let down than when we started.

I then discovered that she and I were on the same flight home back to London, so we shared a taxi to the airport. The atmosphere was frosty.

Then the horror of horrors: we discovered the flight was delayed. She wanted to get some dinner, and said it in such a way it left me with little or no option but to join her.

Any attempts I made at chatting and lightening the mood fell on deaf ears. With much relief, we separated, agreeing to meet up again at the departure gate.

Bearing in mind how the day had gone, I assumed God would have one final joke to play on me, which was to seat us next to each other on the plane.

She boarded well before me, so as I entered the cabin, I hurriedly looked around to see where she was, and working out where her seat was in relation to mine.

Much to my relief, we were rows away from each other, and for the first time since heading off at 6:00 that morning I relaxed.

I was careful to depart the plane as slowly as possible, providing her plenty of time to exit the airport before me, so we didn't need to cross paths.

This was one of my most uncomfortable days at work. Ever.

UNDER PRESSURE: DAVID BOWIE & QUEEN

The most deeply disturbing and stressful period of my career occurred as recently as 2019. Let me set the scene.

I had been at the major American firm since 2016.

The first two years had gone well, I closed some large contracts, and built a strong pipeline. But in year three, some organizational changes resulted in my role changing. And not for the better.

However, despite the new role's challenges, I set out to make it a success.

While I had performed well from a sales point of view during the first two years, the third was a disaster. I ended up way below target.

A week before the Christmas break in 2018, my manager, Marion, sat down with me for a meeting. She informed me that she would need to monitor my performance more formally in the new year.

I deeply resented this. There were valid reasons for the underperformance. Furthermore, I felt the company had failed to back me, despite acknowledging at the outset of that year that the role I had taken on would need up to two years to deliver results. I left for the Christmas break angry.

We reconvened in January and agreed on a compromise. No formal process would be put in place but she would meet with me more frequently and get more involved in customer meetings.

It was a form of truce.

The first quarter of 2019 began full of promise. The foundations I had put in place the previous year began to show results, and my sales pipeline vastly improved.

But it proved to be a false dawn.

By the end of May, sales were still a long way behind target, and the pipeline had been decimated by delays, cancelled projects, and failed bids.

My morale was at an all-time low.

No matter what I did, or how hard I worked, nothing was translating into closed deals.

Furthermore, a feeling of distrust was building up between myself and the firm.

The week before I was due to go on a week's cycling holiday in Tenerife, Marion invited me to a meeting. She informed me that a PIP, a Performance Improvement Plan, would be issued.

For those unfamiliar with the term, it is a recognized UK industry practice applied to employees who are not meeting the required performance or disciplinary standards.

Marion went on to explain that HR would be involved, and we would begin a formal evaluation period, with set targets. If at the end of the process, the plan's targets were not met, then it could result in my dismissal.

While I felt devastated by the decision, it was not a complete surprise.

I left for my week off with a great deal to think about.

There were two ways of looking at the timing of the news and my impending holiday. One view was it was ideal: A chance to clear my head, and get a fresh and clear perspective on what I was facing. The less optimistic view was that it was the last thing I needed. A week off, spent hours and hours cycling every day, with little else to do but get consumed by my thoughts.

As with most things, there turned out to be a bit of good and bad. It did spoil the holiday for me, but also enabled me to decide what I would do on my return.

The way I saw it, there were four options open to me.

Challenge them on the grounds of unfair dismissal.

Resign.

Follow the performance process, or issue the company with a Without Prejudice Compromise letter.

On returning to the UK, I quickly discovered option 1 was not an option, following advice from a law firm. I didn't have another job to go to, so I didn't want to resign, but I didn't want to go through the ignominy and stress of option 3. So I decided on option 4.

For those not familiar with it, the Without Prejudice Compromise letter is issued by either the employer or employee, and expresses a desire to break the employment contract in return for a payment. Employers use them when they want to remove someone but have no clear performance or disciplinary reasons for doing so. The importance of the Compromise method and its legal construct is that if it is agreed to, then the employee waives their right to subsequently claim unfair dismissal.

In my case, as the employee, it was a legal vehicle for offering to resign from a job in return for a payment, and in doing so provide the employer the means to get what they want. Namely the means to get rid of me, while avoiding the overhead of following a Performance Process. It also meant there would be no risk of me, the employee, subsequently claiming unfair dismissal and taking them to court.

My decision to follow this path was driven by a few considerations.

One, I had no wish to work there anyway. I had been looking for a new role, on and off since the beginning of the year.

The second reason was I felt the performance review process was insulting and would be stressful. The memory of my seizure in New York was always on my mind, and the need to avoid undue stress in my life was paramount.

The third was pride. I didn't want to give the company the satisfaction of breaking me and seeing me resign, thereby making it easy for them.

The final reason was I thought the offer of a Compromise Agreement should be appealing to them; it would enable them to avoid the cost and trouble of managing the process over many months.

As you can sense, the "us and them" sentiment had firmly established itself in my thinking.

So, I spent a day or two constructing the offer, wrote the letter, and issued it to HR.

The reply came back a couple of weeks later towards the end of June, by which time I had failed to meet the targets set prior to the cycling trip.

The company rejected my proposal without even offering to negotiate my proposed pay-off terms. Their intent was clear. They wanted rid of me on their terms.

So there we were. I had failed the pre-PIP stage 1 and now I was waiting for the formal process to begin. I had a decision to make, and two of the four options I'd considered were no longer open. I now had to decide whether I reconsider the resignation option, or put myself through the PIP.

The indignity of going through the performance process felt like too much to bear. But the stress was already beginning to affect my health and general wellbeing. Not in a, "I need to be put on Prozac," way, but it was eating away at my confidence and my self-esteem. I was becoming more withdrawn at work, and of course Annie was seeing it at home, with me not "being myself."

I could feel the stress too. Every "ping" of the inbox and the arrival of an email from Marion set off a trigger of "now what" and anxiety.

I remember sitting in the back garden with Annie one evening discussing how I felt, and agreeing the stress was not good for my health. There were two reasons for this.

Obviously, it is not healthy for anyone to endure long periods of stress. A dark cloud had been hanging over my head for over six months already, and to go through another four months or more was neither appealing nor smart. I can endure stressful situations. I have proven this on many occasions. But I knew it wasn't good for me.

The second, which was far more important, links back to the seizure I had in New York two years before. After I returned from New York, I had undergone a range of tests and consultations with the doctors trying to discover the cause. As previously mentioned, the results had been inconclusive; there was no evidence of anything specific that could be treated, and therefore they hoped it was a one-off event. That said, they explained that four factors would increase the likelihood of a recurrence: Taking drugs, having a drink-induced hangover, lack of sleep, and yes, you guessed it, stress. While I am fine on items one and two, I am not a good sleeper, so I didn't want to add stress to the mix.

So Annie and I decided I would resign. My health was more important than my pride, and at that stage, there was little realistic prospect of me getting anywhere near my sales targets.

Perhaps now is a good time to make clear that I have no issue with companies needing to get rid of underperforming salespeople. We all accept this as part of the job.

What I deeply resented was the way they were treating me, and failing to acknowledge and honor the understanding we had when I took on the role; that the role was challenging, it was breaking new ground, and all the salespeople hired before me had failed. It needed a minimum of two years to deliver results.

So having decided to resign, the next decision was when?

There was one deal I had at an advanced stage that held a lot of personal importance for me. I had been working on it for two years, and if it closed it would be a landmark deal for the business unit. I felt it would close within the month, so we agreed I would resign no later than the 31st of July, whether the deal closed or not.

And then someone proposed a different way. I refer to this as my epiphany moment.

It was triggered by a chat over a beer with a friend in the industry. He thought my approach was all wrong, and I shouldn't resign. I should approach each day as a transaction. He explained it like this.

"Employee goes to work; employer pays them for the work. Employee returns the following day, and employer pays them, and so on. Removing the emotion removes the stress. When the arrangement finishes, and the employer no longer wants or needs the employee, then the transaction comes to an end."

And of course he was right. I was allowing my emotions and general state of mind to cloud my thinking. By changing my mindset, I could continue working on my terms, retain my self-respect, and avoid undue stress.

I was worrying too much. It was just a job. Accept the situation for what it was. Don't get emotional, just play the system. They were within their rights to decide they no longer wanted me. These things happen. It was not the first time, and I had recovered each time, usually going on to something better.

So then and there, I decided I would not resign. I would continue to work diligently, but on my terms. I would accept whatever indignities were thrown at me, within reason, and do everything in my power to retain my self-respect. They weren't taking that away from me. No way.

The PIP process began that July and ran through to October. Objectives were set for four-week periods, and my results were reviewed at the end of each period. If I failed to meet the targets, the severity of the consequences increased.

As we worked through the stages, I met all the targets except the one that really counted; the sales target. So I first received a verbal warning, followed by a written warning, followed by a final warning in September. The final period of evaluation would run to October 15. Failure to meet the sales target by that day would result in a dismissal.

While my mindset enabled me to manage most that was thrown at me, there were periods of time I found difficult to manage and stressful. But I was determined to see it through to the end.

I could write a book on the PIP process itself. Suffice to say I found it a charade, and at no time did I feel the company was in any way supportive of me getting through it without being dismissed at the end. The most embarrassing part of it was the conduct of the Senior Vice President of Sales. He would avert his eyes when he passed me in the corridor.

When the final written warning was issued on September 13, 2019, I had reached 20% of the sales target. My target was in excess of $1 million, and I needed to get to at least 80% by the final date of the PIP period.

So, you may be asking, did I have any deals that could possibly sign in time for that target to be met?

Well, as it happens there was one, but it had developed in an unusual manner, and I was in constant denial that it could actually be my savior, my "get out of jail" card.

It started in April as a referral from a client based in Dublin. The subsequent first meeting, in London, went well, and over time the engagement developed in a relatively smooth fashion.

That said, there were plenty of obstacles to overcome.

- The system the client wanted from us was still under development.
- There were no live clients anywhere in the world using it.
- There was a lack of internal support for the product.

- The financial institution we were pitching to was recovering from a scandal that had wiped billions off their balance sheet.
- The system was expensive for what the client wanted to use it for.
- On top of all this, there didn't appear to be any competition under consideration, which is unusual, and made me wary.
- The manager I was dealing with only included one other person in meetings throughout the buying process, so I had little or no visibility of the decision-making process above her. I was therefore anxious that the manager was pursuing the topic without the backing of her directors.
- There was no compelling event; the solution was nice to have.
- Furthermore, if they had wanted to, they could have adopted a similar system they were already licensing from us that could probably have met most of their requirements, and would have cost a fraction of the $1 million I was proposing for the new system.
- Budgets had not been assigned for the initiative, so an exceptional purchase request would have to be raised by them, if they went ahead.

And of course, I was under immense pressure internally, especially with the October 15 date hanging over me like the sword of Damocles.

Putting all of the above aside, I had run a sales process I was proud of, using a range of the skills acquired and refined over the years to good effect. These included:

- A focus on the business drivers, and how a business case for investment could be constructed.
- Developing a bond of trust with the client.
- Persuading the client to accept a limited scope for the proof of concept.
- Successfully selling the opportunity internally, to get resources reassigned in support of the deal.
- Structuring the deal to maximize the overall value, and overcoming the customer objections for a reduced scope.
- Avoiding the need for references being taken up as part of the due diligence.
- Keeping competition out of the bid.

At the point I received my final written warning, legal contracts had been drawn up, the client had reviewed them, and only a dozen or so clauses remained unresolved.

I had just under three weeks to finalize the contracts, get all the necessary approvals, and get the contract signed.

It was tight, but achievable.

However, nagging at the back of my mind was the pricing.

No one at any stage had tried to negotiate my original pricing.

This was unheard of, especially on a $1 million contract.

But what were they waiting for?

Would it happen when it went up for approval from one of the directors?

And surely one of the directors would want to meet me or one of my directors in the normal course of doing business, if they were committing to a $1 million, five-year contract?

What I didn't want to do, of course, was raise the topic myself. But by leaving it as it was, there was a risk it would delay the process, and if they were going to sign, which at this stage was beginning to look quite likely, then I needed it to sign by Tuesday the 15th.

I was also worried by two other things.

As sales processes go, this was one of the most remarkable I had been involved in, when you consider the overall value and the importance of the system. There had been no major setbacks or bumps in the road initiated by the client. All the obstacles I'd overcome had been internal and hidden from the client. As salespeople, we are paranoid. We are always on the lookout for something appearing out of nowhere and crashing a deal. So where and when was it coming, and what would it be?

The other worry was my state of mind. I was very conscious of this, and how it could influence my outlook, decision-making, and general demeanor, any of which could harm the deal.

The week before the 15th, I arranged a conference call between myself, my contact, her legal counsel, and my contracts guy. Prior to the call, I had had to use all my charm and skills of persuasion with my lawyer. He had a reputation for being self-assured, pedantic, and reluctant to negotiate terms that a more pragmatic lawyer would agree to.

However, to his credit, he performed brilliantly and quickly built up a good rapport with the like-minded lawyer representing the bank. Within thirty minutes, all outstanding clauses had been agreed. I couldn't believe it.

Perhaps the gods were looking down on me.

That evening we issued the final drafts. The contracts were agreed, and now just needed sign-off by the client.

I had three working days until the Tuesday. The clock was ticking.

My contact had told me the contract needed approval from two directors. They were already aware of the initiative, and she anticipated a signature within a few days.

My experience of deals like this was vastly different. I was expecting it would require at least a week, more typically two.

If I was to get them on time, I would need her to push hard internally and maybe make a nuisance of herself.

But I couldn't tell her the importance that signing them by Tuesday had for me.

Also, she had told me she would not be in the office on the Monday.

So I left for the weekend expecting the worst.

By Tuesday morning, I had received nothing, so I called the client. One of the directors had signed, she said, and it needed one more. She would go to his office after our call and make sure it was done that day.

I hung up, unsure whether to feel exhilarated or nervous. I decided on a mix of both. The failure to negotiate the prices was still lurking in the back of my mind.

That afternoon I was called into a meeting with Marion.

Our relationship had been chilly at best for over twelve months, and I was in no mood for any more nonsense. I had accepted my fate, I was probably going to be dismissed in due course, and had no wish to talk about my situation anymore.

Furthermore, she had kept her distance for the last few months. She seemed to have given up on me, and felt the need to distance herself from me too.

What followed, however, took me completely by surprise. She let rip on a whole range of matters, criticizing me for this, that and the other, while I ranted back, giving as good as I got. As we brought the meeting to a close, she commented, "Well, as far as I can see, Michael, whichever way you look at it, prospects don't look very good for you."

By this time, I was fuming. So, I lifted my wrist, and with dramatic effect, looked down, and said: "Well, Marion, according to my watch, there are still over two hours left of the day, so let's see what happens, shall we? You never know, when I return to my desk, the signed deal may be sitting in my inbox!!"

And lo and behold, there it was. Signed, sealed, and delivered. A $1 million contract.

Her reaction to the news was understated, as was the reaction of her boss and the Senior Vice President of Sales. I think they were all shocked, not believing the deal would actually happen, and in such dramatic fashion.

The only response I got was a one-line, "Well done" email.

I didn't care. Whatever happened now, I would walk away with my head held high, my self-respect and reputation firmly secured, and an irrefutable statement that showed I met and exceeded the sales target set for that year.

That evening, over a celebration bottle of champagne with Annie, I began wondering whether or not this deal that I had "pulled out of a hat" at the last minute would actually be enough to stop them dismissing me. It would be tough for them to do so, according to UK legislation, but if there was a way, I knew they would want to.

To cut a long story short, Marion invited me to a meeting a week later, and shared with me the decision. I would not be sacked.

That said, all the disciplinary warnings would remain on my personnel record for two years, and I could not be considered for any new internal roles during that time.

By the end of the year, I closed two more new contracts, I finished the year on over 130% of target, and my commission check was paid in the December salary run. On January 2, 2020, I resigned to start my own sales consultancy, with the biggest smile on my face you can imagine.

I could of course have stayed at the company, but there were too many reasons against it. I knew starting my own business was a risk, and I was sacrificing a regular monthly salary, but I didn't care. I had earned the right to peace of mind, and by this time, that far outweighed any potential financial considerations.

Within a couple of months, Covid-19 was sweeping through the world, we were all in lockdown, and I had a business barely a month old.

But that's another story, for another time.

About the Author

Michael is a professional B2B salesperson, running his own sales consultancy practice, built on the foundations of a thirty-year track record in technology sales into the financial banking sector.

Prior to this, in the 1980s he had two specialist crossword books published, one entitled *Rock and Pop Crosswords*, and the follow-up entitled *Telly Teasers Crossword Puzzles*.

Michael lives in London, England, with his wife Annie and two adorable cats, Ruby and Frank.

References

Muir, James M. 2016. *The Perfect Close*. 1st ed. Utah: Best Practice International.

Konrath, Jill. 2012. *SNAP Selling*. 1st ed. New York City: Portfolio, Penguin Group.

Rackham, Neil. 2001. *SPIN Selling*. New ed. UK: Hampshire: Gower Publishing.

Kahneman, Daniel. 2012. *Thinking, Fast and Slow*. New ed. UK: Penguin Random House.

Carnegie, Dale. 2022. *How To Win Friends And Influence People*. New ed. New York: Simon & Schuster.

Collis, Ray & Gorman, John, O. 2010. *The B2B Sales Revolution*. 1st ed. Dublin: The ASG Group.

Dixon, Matthew & Adamson, Brent. 2011. *The Challenger Sale*. 1st ed. New York: Penguin Group.

Miller, Robert B & Heiman, Stephen E. 1985. *Strategic Selling*. 1st ed. New York: William Morrow & Co.

Sobczak, Art. 1996. *Telephone Tips That Sell*. 1st ed. Arizona: Business By Phone.

Sobczak, Art. 2020. *Smart Calling: Eliminate The Fear, Failure and Rejection From Cold Calling.* 3rd ed. New Jersey: John Wiley & Sons.

Other:

Corporate Visions Webinars: host Tim Riesterer

The Art of Sales Podcast: host Art Sobczak

A free ebook edition is available with the purchase of this book.

To claim your free ebook edition:

1. Visit MorganJamesBOGO.com
2. Sign your name CLEARLY in the space
3. Complete the form and submit a photo of the entire copyright page
4. You or your friend can download the ebook to your preferred device

A **FREE** ebook edition is available for you or a friend with the purchase of this print book.

CLEARLY SIGN YOUR NAME ABOVE

Instructions to claim your free ebook edition:
1. Visit MorganJamesBOGO.com
2. Sign your name CLEARLY in the space above
3. Complete the form and submit a photo of this entire page
4. You or your friend can download the ebook to your preferred device

Print & Digital Together Forever.

Snap a photo

Free ebook

Read anywhere